10th e-Learning Excellence Awards 2024

An Anthology of Case Histories

Edited by Dan Remenyi

10th e-Learning Excellence Awards: An Anthology of Case Histories

Copyright © 2024 The authors

First published October 2024

All rights reserved. Except for the quotation of short passages for the purposes of critical review, no part of this publication may be reproduced in any material form (including photocopying or storing in any medium by electronic means and whether or not transiently or incidentally to some other use of this publication) without the written permission of the copyright holder except in accordance with the provisions of the Copyright Designs and Patents Act 1988, or under the terms of a licence issued by the Copyright Licensing Agency Ltd, Saffron House, 6-10 Kirby Street, London EC1N 8TS. Applications for the copyright holder's written permission to reproduce any part of this publication should be addressed to the publishers.

Disclaimer: While every effort has been made by the editor, authors and the publishers to ensure that all the material in this book is accurate and correct at the time of going to press, any error made by readers as a result of any of the material, formulae or other information in this book is the sole responsibility of the reader. Readers should be aware that the URLs quoted in the book may change or be damaged by malware between the time of publishing and accessing by readers.

Note to readers: Some papers have been written by authors who use the American form of spelling and some use the British. These two different approaches have been left unchanged.

ISBN: 978-1-917204-16-3 (Print)
ISBN: 978-1-917204-17-0 (pdf)

Published by: Academic Conferences International Limited, Reading, United Kingdom, info@academic-conferences.org

Available from www.academic-bookshop.com

Contents

Acknowledgements iv

Introduction v

Micromate: Integrating Sustainable and Easy-to-Use Digital Learning into Employees' Daily Routines 1
    Christoph Süess and Lena Zeigang

Strengthening Hong Kong Educators: Integrating Blended Learning with Technological Advancements 15
    Paul Lam, Carmen Lau, Man Tsang, Theresa Kwong, Grace Ng, Kendall Yan

BP4WE: Best Practices for Workgroup E-assessment with Web AVALIA 29
    Rosalina Babo

GreenCool Online and Blended Learning MOOC 39
    Edit Kővári, Anastasiia Turusinova and Réka Vámosi

Simulating the Complex Science Behind Environmental Hazards Like Post-wildfire Debris Flows 55
    Keliann LaConte, Vanessa Vincente and James Russell

XP Boost: Empowering Generation Alpha's Food Literacy 71
    Nadine du Piesanie, Nadene Marx-Pienaar, Nadine Sonnenberg and Adeline Pretorius

Utilzing Mobile Learning and Gamification to Control Tobacco Use in India" ... 85
    Eve M. Nagler, Chuck Sigmund, Priyanka Ghosh, Smita P. Warke, Leah C. Jones, Paromita Mehta, Samhita Kalidindi, Mangesh S. Pednekar

Using Gamification and Artificial Intelligence to Increase Learning Effectiveness and Motivation 95
    Lam Tai Lee

Acknowledgements

We would like to thank the judges, who initially read the abstracts of the case histories submitted to the competition and discussed these to select those to be submitted as full case histories. They subsequently performed double-blind evaluations of the entries and made further selections to produce the finalists who are published in this book.

Paula Charbonneau Gowdy is Associate Professor in English as a Foreign Language Teacher Education at the Universidad Andres Bello in Santiago, Chile and formerly Senior Advisor in Learning and Technology to the Government of Canada. Her research interests lie in the sociocultural implications of online learning for teaching, learning and learners.

Susan Crichton is an emeritus professor in Educational Technologies at the University of British Columbia, Canada. She is currently a consultant who has been working to support educators in the K-12 sector, as well as post-secondary trades training and university to respond to the challenges posed by COVID 19.

Colin Loughlin is the Learning Technology Manager at the University of Surrey (UK) and a PhD candidate with Lund University (Sweden). His research interests are related to large class teaching and the impact of educational theory on classroom practice. Recently published: 'Reclaiming Constructive Alignment' (bit.ly/reclaimingCA)

Shawren Singh is an Associate Professor at the School of Computing at the University of South Africa, he has spent more than 20 years teaching and researching in the Information Systems space. In 2014 he obtained his PhD, based on research into eGovernment in South Africa, from the University of the Witwatersrand. His current research has focused on digital scholarship and e-Government, his research has been published internationally and he has presented papers at several conferences.

Introduction

e-Learning, along with blended learning, has become an essential and widely adopted method for delivering education and training at all levels, including in the workplace. The International e-Learning Excellence Awards offer a platform for individuals and teams to explore and showcase innovative approaches to this mode of learning.

This year's response to the tenth International e-Learning Excellence Awards demonstrates the ongoing creativity in e-learning across the globe. With 22 initial submissions from 10 different countries, 18 competitors were invited to submit detailed case histories outlining their initiatives. The case histories covered a broad range of topics, making it a challenging task for the panel of expert judges, who conducted a blind review to identify the most compelling submissions and narrow them down to the finalists featured in this anthology.

Eight authors or groups of authors have been invited to present their work in the final rounds of this competition at the 2024 European Conference on e-Learning, being held at the University of Portucalense, Porto, Portugal, and as finalists these initiatives are published in this book of case histories. The topics to be addressed are listed in the Contents page of this book and represent projects from Hong Kong, Hungary, India. Kingdom of Saudi Arabia, Portugal, South Africa, Switzerland and the United States.

I would like to thank all the contributors to the book for the excellent work which has been done towards developing new and interesting ways of applying e-Learning. And of course, it is also important to thank the individuals who constituted our panel of expert judges.

Dr Dan Remenyi
October 2024

Micromate: Integrating Sustainable and Easy-to-Use Digital Learning into Employees' Daily Routines

Christoph Süess and Lena Zeigang
Paixon GmbH, Zurich, Switzerland
christoph.sueess@micromate.ai,
lena.zeifang@micromate.ai

Abstract: Nowadays, in a fast-paced work environment (Frémeaux & Henry, 2023), organizations face several changes in managing learning. Technology transformed education and resulted in new concepts of learning that have been influenced by technological advancements and the demands and needs towards individualization by individuals. Thus, employees require new ways of learning (Baz, 2018). Especially to cope with the digital transformation successfully, the continuous development of skills and competencies is crucial for organizations to remain attractive as an employer and to stay competitive in the market (Meier et al., 2024). Micromate is a conversational e-learning assistant that integrates seamlessly into existing learning or work environments. Micromate deepens knowledge by conducting quizzes in microlearning sessions through natural-sounding chat conversations. Consequently, Micromate represents a minimal obstacle to employees' acquisition of knowledge during brief interludes in their daily activities. Micromate simultaneously offers the potential for employees to invest a mere five minutes in learning activities within their already demanding schedules, with straightforward access and an intuitive design. Looking ahead, Micromate aims to be not only a daily partner for continuous learning but also a companion in identifying knowledge gaps and recommending personalized learning paths. This will help organizations achieve optimal development in corporate learning, driving entrepreneurial success.

Keywords: E-Learning, Microlearning, Conversational Learning, Personalized Learning, Corporate Learning

1. Introduction

Already in June 1990 at his speech at Madison Park High School in Boston, Nelson Mandela (1918-2013) once said, *"Education is the most powerful weapon which you can use to change the world."*. Nowadays, corporations face change continuously. Due to trends like digitalization or artificial intelligence (AI), the environment where companies are located gets more complex and less predictable, hence the capability of renewal becomes imperative. Therefore, learning is essential. Experiential learning, continuous reflection, and effective knowledge management are crucial for maintaining competitiveness (Kels et al., 2024). To remain competitive (Meier et al., 2024), organizations must continuously develop employee competencies.

Technological changes associated with the Fourth Industrial Revolution are also transforming education, requiring more individualized and interactive approaches to employee development (Sakhapov & Absalyamova, 2018). Where traditional learning approaches come with limitations (Hug, 2022), today's requirements by employees can be addressed by easier concepts and transformative tools like microlearning (Samala et al., 2023).

Recognizing the need for easily accessible and quick learning options for employees, the founders of Micromate, Christoph Süess and Stefan Schöb, who initially established Paixon GmbH to develop chatbot projects, discovered a niche in e-learning. They saw the potential for chatbots in both, the external communication with chatbots and their internal application within organizations. Since 2021, the team has been developing the software Micromate in-house. By 2023, Micromate became their main focus, involving almost all employees of Paixon GmbH. In 2023, Micromate was promoted and launched publicly via social media. By the end of 2024, the conversational assistant is expected to be further developed to enhance corporate learning with a digital assistant.

Micromate is a software application that conducts microlearning quizzes in chat conversations. By that, learning sessions are conducted in conversations with Micromate. In each learning session, five questions are presented to the learner in a personalized manner, based on an algorithm. These questions are in the form of single, multiple, true/false, or open-ended formats. Micromate is not supposed to be a stand-alone application, but to be integrated into existing learning environments or learning management systems (LMS) that are platforms where learners get access to learning content (Şahin & Yurdugül, 2022, p. 33). By that, hurdles associated with multiple applications and tools shall be overcome and make learning a part of nowadays daily routines within corporate settings.

Especially this integration into existing learning environments distinguishes Micromate from other applications. Thus, companies and their employees do not need additional logins or user data to use and access Micromate but can use and learn with "**Learn Micromate**" in their existing learning environment or communication channel through implementations or plug-ins.

"**Manage Micromate**" provides a platform for employees or managers who are responsible for learning within organizations and offers a simple platform for managing the content, groups, and learners.

"**Micromate AI**" provides additional support to managers in content generation and reduces learner inquiries as the feature provides the ability to submit questions to Micromate that will be answered by Micromate. "Micromate AI" only references validated and approved resources.

Learn Micromate is excelling in user-friendliness for learners and managers due to intuitive learning in conversations. It is an easy approach and that seeks to motivate employees to learn continuously and by individual learning paths, based on an algorithm. Gamification is supposed to increase engagement by rewards through badges, rankings, and goal achievement. These features are based on concepts of social theory, a concept that comprehends social interactions in online learning settings (Dasgupta, 2010) that Micromate is applying through features such as rankings. Furthermore, concepts like the agency theory (Shapiro, 2005), where Micromate takes over the role of an agent to ensure an effective learning approach in organizations that face changes like higher demand for individualization, interaction, or virtualization as a result of a digital environment (Sakhapov & Absalyamova, 2018), are applied.

Micromate already achieved successful showcases, indicating its effectiveness in corporate learning as well as in universities. The customer-oriented approach and development of Micromate allows continuous improvement and adaptation of the application and lays the foundation for an application able to cope with the real-world challenges of corporates. Micromate therefore plans to further support employees and managers by identifying skill gaps, making individual recommendations, and enhancing social learning in the future.

2. Infrastructure

Micromate is an application featuring a frontend for learners (**Learn Micromate**) and a backend for managers (**Manage Micromate**). Both are accessible over the internet. Nevertheless, the frontend of Micromate is also available as a Microsoft Teams (MS) App. Additionally, individual developments can be done to integrate Micromate into existing applications and learning environments such as learning management systems like Moodle.

Application Programming Interfaces (APIs) enable the option to communicate with other applications. Figure 1 illustrates the logic of Micromate.

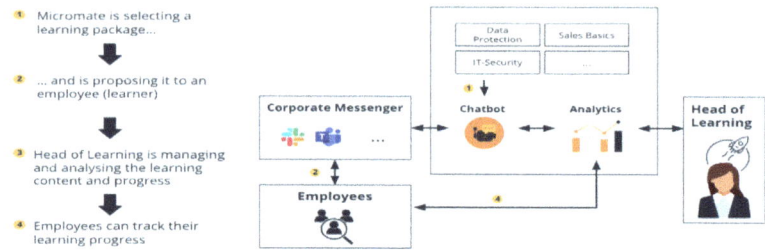

Figure 1: Logic of Micromate; Source: Slides product presentation Micromate

Micromate has been developed in Switzerland. Thus, the whole application is hosted in Switzerland too. Micromate considers the Data Protection Act (FADP), and General Data Protection Regulation (GDPR). Hence, the application is aligned and fulfills high standards in security.

The frontend application "Learn Micromate" can be used via the browser, MS Teams, or can be integrated into a learning or work environment of choice. Organized into different tabs, the chat conversation (shown in Figure 2) with Micromate is the main section of the application. In the chat, microlearning sessions which consist of quizzes with 5 questions are conducted and displayed individualized by an algorithm that considers concepts such as Ebbinghaus's forgetting curve (1998), where repetition influences learners' memory. The other tabs provide access to gamification features like badges (shown in Figure 2) that are issued along the conversation and extended by social ranking to compete. These concepts are also based on conducted research and proposals by Benner et al. (Benner et al., 2022). The learning progress indicator shows the current knowledge level, promoting continuous learning through a dynamic system where ceasing to learn results in a decline in learning status.

Figure 2: Chat conversation with Micromate and badges (Gamification); Source: Learn Micromate

"Micromate AI" allows employees to ask questions. Micromate AI uses Large Language Models (LLMs) (Teubner et al., 2023) from Open AI as a general infrastructure provider. Nevertheless, Micromate also offers to connect to a company's LLMs to ensure more data privacy and minimize risk. Micromate AI is also available for "Manage Micromate" to generate content. The challenges faced by managers are given particular focus in this context, as they are characterized by minimal time resources. Therefore, content generation and translations are supported by AI.

"Manage Micromate" is an intuitive backend for managers. It is the administration platform where content is created and allocated to learners, meaning employees, either manually or by linkages to existing systems in which, for example, user access is managed. "Manage Micromate" consists of three areas which are the learning center, the editor, and the area of analytics. In the learning center, groups and learning content can be managed. In the editor section, content is generated and managed, and finally, the analytics section allows for insights, whilst protecting individuals and still providing valuable insights for improvements of learning content. Figure 3 shows an overview of the editor, where learning content can be managed by for example manually generating questions or editing, tagging or translating them.

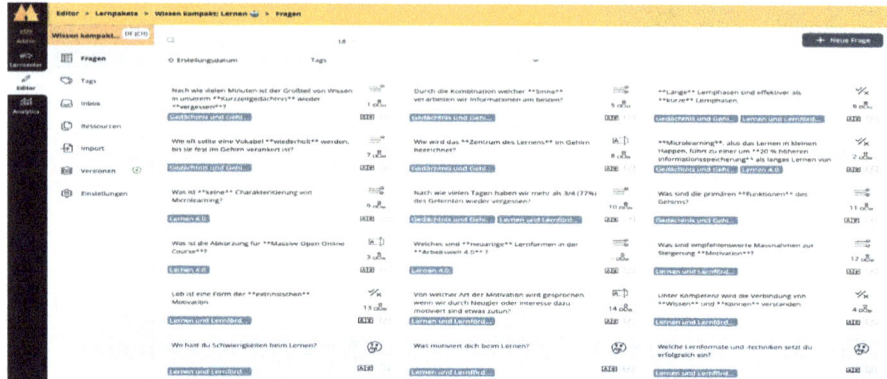

Figure 3: Manage Micromate Insight into the Editor; Source: Manage Micromate

To date, more than 2,300,000 questions have been answered by over 4,000 learners using Micromate. Currently, around 1,300 people actively use Micromate each month, answering over 200,000 questions across more than 300 learning packages.

We believe that without a strong team, software is useless. Fortunately, Micromate has a strong and diverse team of five individuals. Four team members have a computer science background, and one has a business administration background. Our team members have valuable knowledge in software development, design, user perception, and computer linguistics, ensuring they possess all the necessary skills to develop chat-based learning software. The company was originally founded to develop individual software projects for chat and voice bots, providing existing knowledge on the complexity of conversational agents (CAs), such as chatbots (Schindler et al., 2024), along with entrepreneurial experience.

At Micromate, structured processes ensure quality in the software and customer experience. Therefore, Micromate adopts a partner-like approach with clients, actively incorporating their continuous feedback through close collaboration.

Through this collaborative approach and by working closely with customers, the experienced and skilled team established a ready-to-use application that is available as an MS Teams App, as stand-alone software, and can be integrated into existing environments with APIs. AI features increase efficiency and responsiveness and solve challenges mentioned by customers. Nevertheless, the team has a compelling vision and is striving towards an international expansion of Micromate across Europe by 2029 to revolutionize corporate learning by integrating digital learning into employees' daily routines. As of today, customers are mainly located in Switzerland, Germany, and Austria.

3. Challenges

The development of a compelling, user-oriented, and high-quality software application does not come without challenges. These obstacles include continuous development for customers and entrepreneurial challenges faced by a young entrepreneurial team.

In business-to-business (B2B) relationships, particularly with companies having multiple stakeholders, implementing a software application is a significant decision. Change management, implementation, adjustments, and internal processes increase the complexity and the requirements, hence making the development more complex and generating entrepreneurial and leadership challenges due to increasing pressure on existing resources such as staff, infrastructure, and financing. Nevertheless, the challenges and strategies to overcome them are presented and categorized into two main areas:

1. Growth and Customer Acquisition
2. Operational Efficiency and Sustainability

Growth and Customer Acquisition: Acquiring customers in the Business-to-Business (B2B) environment has been challenging. Since Micromate successfully acquired several larger companies (each with more than 2,000 employees), the software had to be adjusted and extended to align with their needs. Requirements are often high, with companies demanding adherence to specific quality standards and guidelines, such as corporate branding, security protocols, and implementation plans.

However, the team has successfully met these needs by evaluating trends in corporate learning and finding innovative, smart solutions that deliver value to customers.

Operational Efficiency and Sustainability: The team working on Micromate is small, yet multiple tasks need to be done. Also, with time and an increasing demand, the team has grown. This required the establishment of new structures, processes, and alignment within the development of the application as well as daily business operations. Hence, it also required a visionary leadership approach, still providing employees enough freedom to tackle a high number of tasks and maintain high quality in technology and customer service.

Furthermore, Micromate is bootstrapped without external funding. Due to increasing demand for employees working on this project, resulted in a challenge to reduce bootstrapping to a minimum while covering the expenses with Micromate license revenues.

Still, by giving employees responsibilities, defining clear processes and structuring our work style, operational efficiency, and sustainability have been tackled successfully. Agile approaches like daily standup meetings, for example, provide a clear structure and customer orientation while still providing flexibility and continuous communication.

4. First Results and Experiences

Over the last two years, positive feedback has proven the need and effectiveness of Micromate, with successful cases in diverse industries and settings. A major success case to be mentioned is the usage of Micromate at Helvetia Versicherungen Switzerland. While starting in their service center with more than 100 employees, the engagement was to be admired, and hence today, in different pilot projects more than 1,000 employees at Helvetia already could learn with Micromate. The key to success, as told by the manager of the project, was the integration of Micromate in MS Teams and thus the direct embedding in a daily work tool, making it possible for employees to learn along their busy and fast-changing work environment in the insurance industry.

Furthermore, Swiss Unihockey, a Swiss national sport, is exploring new learning methods by applying Micromate across their entire organization. Specifically, each year, 1,600 referees are trained and receive their certificates as arbitrators through Micromate. This new approach and the elimination of audits are regarded as extremely positive and sustainable by both administrators and referees.

A third proof of concept, in addition to multiple other use cases where Micromate is used, has been demonstrated by applying Micromate in a university context. During the semester, students had the opportunity to deepen their class knowledge with Micromate. As a result, the average scores of students who prepared for exams with Micromate increased (Russ, 2021). While universities are not the usual setting for Micromate, this has shown its effectiveness also in other fields or realms. Close relationships with universities have been instrumental in testing and scientifically developing Micromate further, resulting in multiple projects.

The first initial project conducted in 2018 was an "Innosuisse Innovationsscheck". This project, sponsored by Innosuisse, researched how organizational learning with messenger chatbots can be achieved. As a result of the project, Micromate has been identified as an important module to support lifelong learning. As Micromate has been tested in two companies along the project, its market potential was identified and thus further pursued, as the pilot study indicated that chatbots can be well integrated into the management of organizational knowledge and thereby excel in simplicity.

Building on the identified potential, an 18-month Innosuisse research project titled 'Micromate - Lernförderung Durch Digitalen Lernassistenten' was undertaken. Collaborating with researchers from the Lucerne University of Applied Sciences (HSLU) and Zürcher Hochschule für Angewandte Wissenschaften (ZHAW), Micromate was tested and examined both qualitatively and quantitatively. The project investigated employee trust in chatbots using the technology acceptance model (TAM) (Davis, 1989). The findings were presented at the FINT Conference in Helsinki (Leppälä & Snellman, 2023, p. 26). Researchers from ZHAW also focused on integrating Micromate into organizational culture, gamification elements, and designing learning assistants for successful implementation. Figure 4 shows the study design by ZHAW.

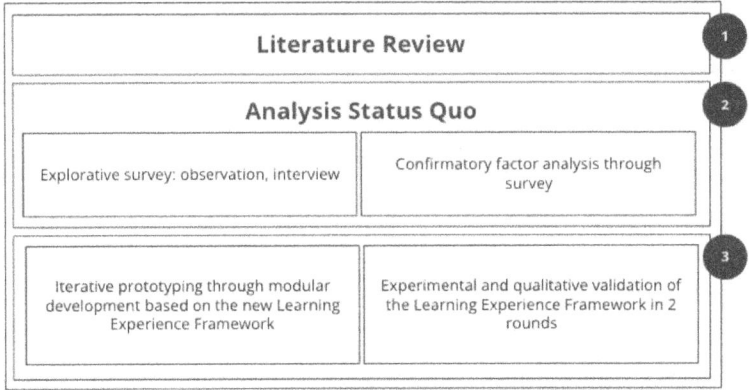

Figure 4: Study Design Innosuisse Project

Source: Adapted slide from Dr. Wolfgang Schäfer, ZHAW

As a result of the study done by ZHAW, the needs of organizations and employees have been able to be identified to improve Micromate.

5. The Learning Outcomes

As of today, more than 2,300,000 questions have been answered. 1,300 learners have engaged with Micromate in the last 30 days while more than 4,000 already tested and learned at least once with the application. By conducting in total more than 460,000 learning sessions with 5 questions each session, employees and individuals have been impressively engaging with Micromate.

The numbers speak for themselves, conducted user evaluations feedback meetings, and workshops with clients additionally proof the successful learning outcomes. In a survey, almost 300 participants gave valuable insights, showing that they mainly learn with Micromate over their smartphone (69.9%), evaluate Micromate as useful for learning (Likert scale 1-7; 81.6% ranging from 5-7), and assess it as enjoyable to learn with Micromate (Likert scale 1-7; 75% ranging from 4-7). Especially qualitative responses indicated the importance of gamification, the commitment to the simplicity of Micromate and the assessment that the application is fast, simple, and uncomplicated.

Except for regular feedback from customers, we internally apply the concept of dogfooding to ensure qualitative development of Micromate and ensuring functionality, minimizing bugs, and delivering functional software to achieve maximum customer satisfaction.

6. Plans for further development

Micromate is a ready-to-use software with multiple interfaces, customization options, and various features. We continuously monitor trends and needs to further adjust and enhance the application.

1. **Micromate AI:** As "Micromate AI" has been released in May 2023, the continuous improvement to enhance the capabilities and quality of Micromate AI is one of our ongoing tasks. Further supporting content creation by AI and simplifying and speeding up the creation of content is one specific plan for further development that we are already working on.
2. **Voice-Based Learning:** Recognizing the need for learning in non-office environments, we are planning in developing voice-based learning options. This will facilitate learning in areas such as manufacturing or while commuting.
3. **Social Learning and User-Generated Content:** We value collaboration and knowledge sharing within organizations. Therefore, we plan to add social learning features and empower employees to

contribute to content creation, enhancing knowledge transfer and engagement.
4. Individualization and Knowledge Gap Discovery: What matters is the individual, their strengths and skills, and also their weaknesses. As Micromate already individualizes the questions and their appearance based on an algorithm, in the future further individualization and recommendations are planned to propose suitable topics or times for learning. By adding a knowledge gap discovery feature, individuals are supposed to be supported by Micromate to discover and propose the skills they need, ensuring and enhancing their individual professional development.

7. Conclusion

In the fast-paced business world where companies are located in an ever-changing environment, the need for personalized, bite-sized, and sustainable options for self-guided learning becomes imperative. Hence, Micromate represents a compelling and customer-oriented approach to enhance corporate learning and to shape the outdated learning environments of organizations into employee-geared ones adapted to the future, whilst minimizing effort for learners and managers and lowering hurdles for access and continuous learning towards employees' individual needs.

Micromate is simple, self-explanatory, and continuously available. Especially through the possible integration into any type of existing learning environment, the tool landscape of companies does not expand unnecessarily and confusingly but is still complemented by small, everyday-friendly extensions.

To sum up, Micromate has proven to be an effective application for the challenges that organizations face in corporate learning today. By introducing Micromate, companies can ensure their employees' knowledge remains current without interrupting daily tasks, creating a sustainable and efficient learning environment that supports individual development and organizational success

References

Benner, D., Schöbel, S., Süess, C., Baechle, V., & Janson, A. (2022). *Level-Up your Learning – Introducing a Framework for Gamified Educational Conversational Agents*. 17th International Conference on Wirtschaftsinformatik, Nürnberg.

Dasgupta, S. (Ed.). (2010). *Social Computing: Concepts, Methodologies, Tools, and Applications*. IGI Global. https://doi.org/10.4018/978-1-60566-984-7

Davis, F. D. (1989). Perceived Usefulness, Perceived Ease Of Use, And User Acceptance of Information Technology. *MIS Quarterly*, *13*(3), 319–340.

Ebbinghaus, H. (1998). Memory: A contribution to experimental psychology. Thoemmes.

Frémeaux, S., & Henry, F. (2023). Temporality and Meaningful Entrepreneurship. *Journal of Business Ethics*, *188*(4), 725–739. https://doi.org/10.1007/s10551-023-05502-0

Hug, T. (2022). Microlearning Formats in Crisis? Theses in the Field of Tension Between Corona-Induced Short-Term Solutions, Apodictic Rhetoric's of no Alternatives and Perspectives Open to the Future. In E. Smyrnova-Trybulska, P. Kommers, M. Drlík, & J. Skalka (Eds.), *Microlearning* (pp. 125–139). Springer International Publishing. https://doi.org/10.1007/978-3-031-13359-6_8

Kels, P., Kocher, P.-Y., Decker, V. M., Haldemann, R., & Senn, P. (2024). Die erneuerungsfähige Organisation. *Zfo - Zeitschrift Führung Und Organisation*, *2*, 120–124.

Leppälä, K., & Snellman, K. (2023). FINT 2023 12th Workshop and Doctoral Colloquium—Trust Within and Between Organizations. University of Eastern Finland.

Meier, J.-M., Meyer, M., Geiger, M., Robra-Bissantz, S., & Triltsch, U. (2024). Digitale Kompetenzen in der Weiterbildung: Gestaltung eines praxiszentrierten Weiterbildungskonzeptes für KMU. *HMD Praxis der Wirtschaftsinformatik*, *61*(1), 175–188. https://doi.org/10.1365/s40702-023-01038-z

Micromate—Lernförderung durch digitalen Lernassistenten. (n.d.). Retrieved 28 June 2024, from https://www.hslu.ch/de-ch/hochschule-luzern/forschung/projekte/detail/?pid=6020

Russ, C. (2021). *Https://blog.zhaw.ch/winsights/2021/10/04/verbessertes-micro-learning-von-itil-fachwissen-mittels-chat-bot/*. https://blog.zhaw.ch/winsights/2021/10/04/verbessertes-micro-learning-von-itil-fachwissen-mittels-chat-bot/

Şahin, M., & Yurdugül, H. (2022). Learners' Needs in Online Learning Environments and Third Generation Learning Management Systems (LMS 3.0). *Technology, Knowledge and Learning*, *27*(1), 33–48. https://doi.org/10.1007/s10758-020-09479-x

Sakhapov, R., & Absalyamova, S. (2018). Fourth industrial revolution and the paradigm change in engineering education. *MATEC Web of Conferences*, *245*, 12003. https://doi.org/10.1051/matecconf/201824512003

Samala, A. D., Bojic, L., Bekiroğlu, D., Watrianthos, R., & Hendriyani, Y. (2023). Microlearning: Transforming Education with Bite-Sized Learning on the Go—Insights and Applications. *International Journal of Interactive Mobile Technologies (iJIM)*, *17*(21), 4–24. https://doi.org/10.3991/ijim.v17i21.42951

Schindler, D., Maiberger, T., Koschate-Fischer, N., & Hoyer, W. D. (2024). How speaking versus writing to conversational agents shapes consumers' choice and choice satisfaction. *Journal of the Academy of Marketing Science*, *52*(3), 634–652. https://doi.org/10.1007/s11747-023-00987-7

Shapiro, S. P. (2005). Agency Theory. *Annual Review of Sociology*, *31*(1), 263–284. https://doi.org/10.1146/annurev.soc.31.041304.122159

Teubner, T., Flath, C. M., Weinhardt, C., Van Der Aalst, W., & Hinz, O. (2023). Welcome to the Era of ChatGPT et al.: The Prospects of Large Language Models. *Business & Information Systems Engineering*, *65*(2), 95–101. https://doi.org/10.1007/s12599-023-00795-x

Author biographies

Christoph Süess, CEO Paixon GmbH & Founder of Micromate, studied software development and worked as a software engineer. He founded his own venture in 2015. His company Paixon GmbH has been developing software projects for chatbots and voice bots. He is one of two founders of Micromate and is working as managing director

Lena Zeifang, Customer Success Manager at Micromate, studied business administration for her bachelor's and is currently studying business administration for her master's degree. Since 2022, Lena has been supporting Micromate in business development, marketing, communications, and as a customer success manager.

Strengthening Hong Kong Educators: Integrating Blended Learning with Technological Advancements

Paul Lam[1], Carmen Lau1, Man Tsang[1], Theresa Kwong[2], Grace Ng[2], and Kendall Yan[2]
[1]Centre for Learning Enhancement and Research, The Chinese University of Hong Kong
[2]Centre for Holistic Teaching and Learning, Hong Kong Baptist University
paul.lam@cuhk.edu.hk
carmenlau@cuhk.edu.hk
manstang@cuhk.edu.hk

Abstract: The rapid adoption of blended learning in response to the Covid-19 has significantly transformed Hong Kong's educational landscape, affecting educators, administrators, students, and their families. Teachers had to quickly transition from traditional to blended learning. This sudden shift involved not just a change in teaching methods but also the development and maintenance of digital content and the modification of classroom techniques, leading to increased workload and stress. For students, especially the younger ones, the challenge lay in moving from a structured, teacher-led framework to one that demanded more self-regulation. To tackle these challenges, our project (known as the Jockey Club "Blended Learning" Project) introduced the Blended Learning Innovations Support Scheme (BLISS) for all primary and secondary teachers in Hong Kong. BLISS provided professional pedagogical consultation, guiding teachers to use blended learning strategies to design effective lessons. Additionally, we offered a Peer-mentor Training Programme and a Certification Course that prepared experienced teachers to support their colleagues and foster a collaborative co-learning culture. A school leader committee was established to develop and share blended learning management strategies, thus ensuring administrative backing. We also conducted parent workshops to enhance their participation in blended learning, providing them with tools to support their children's independent learning. To support students, we launched the "BLISS Self-Learning Platform," an e-learning hub with free and open instructional videos and exercises to promote self-study. Recognizing Generative AI's revolutionary role, we initiated training for teachers to harness AI in education, with sessions led by ed-tech experts and frontline teachers. BLISS has reached over 400 teachers across 71 partner schools, benefiting 9,200 students with trial blended learning experiences and generating promising early results. The effectiveness of our project is profound, as supported by the feedback collected from our first-year engagement surveys and interviews with teachers and students from partner schools. A resounding 83% of teachers confirmed their understanding of blended learning

e-Learning Excellence Awards

has significantly enhanced, while 80% reported an increased level of confidence in implementing blended learning strategies.

1. Introduction

The Covid-19 pandemic precipitated an unprecedented, widespread shift to online learning, marking a dramatic transformation in educational delivery and development. This rapid transition exposed significant unpreparedness within the education sector, leading to varying degrees of stress, anxiety, and emotional distress among teachers and students in Hong Kong as they navigated new learning environments (Yeung & Yau, 2021; Moorhouse, 2021). The shift from a "passive" to an "active" learning model challenges the traditional "spoon-feeding" approach prevalent in Hong Kong's education system, which has been criticized for promoting rote and passive learning. Blended learning redefines the student's role to that of an active knowledge seeker, requiring a higher degree of ownership and self-direction in their learning journey—a stark departure from the passive absorption traditionally encouraged (Sharma, 2019).

As a result of these changes, teachers felt pressured to reinvent their teaching methods, which included developing and maintaining digital content and modifying classroom techniques, subsequently increasing their workloads and stress levels. For students, especially the younger ones, the challenge lied in moving from a structured, teacher-led framework to one that demanded more self-guidance. Parents, too, were affected as they needed to familiarize themselves with the digital tools used in blended learning. Increased parental involvement was required for supervising online learning and supporting self-directed learning, which could be particularly challenging for working parents.

Acknowledging the challenges presented by the shift to blended learning, the Jockey Club "Blended Learning Project" is designed to develop effective support systems to alleviate the burden on educators, assist students during their transition, and empower parents to manage their new roles more effectively.

Our primary objective is to cultivate a sustainable digital strategy in Hong Kong schools, emphasizing blended learning and self-directed learning to address the evolving educational challenges presented by the new normal. Our approach distinguishes us from other initiatives as we utilize both top-down and bottom-up strategies to drive meaningful transformational and organizational changes in education. We actively involve school leaders in discussions about teaching innovations, empowering them to implement their own strategies for pedagogical improvement. Simultaneously, we provide comprehensive support to teachers, students, and parents through lesson study sessions and enrichment activities, promoting a sense of ownership, self-empowerment, and mutual support.

With this strategic vision in mind, our project is structured around three key objectives:

1. Empower Teachers: It is important to provide teachers with the necessary tools, knowledge, skills, and peer support to implement blended learning effectively. This objective is achieved through targeted professional development programs, access to a comprehensive suite of teaching and learning resources, and the formation of a supportive community of practice.

2. Support Students: We strive to offer assistance for students who may struggle in blended learning due to low motivation and slow learning pace. We provide a digital platform with self-learning resources and interactive features to ensure that all students can benefit from and engage with blended learning environments.

3. Engage Stakeholders: We aim to increase the acceptance and support for blended learning among various stakeholders, particularly school leaders and parents. This involves outreach initiatives, informational workshops, and collaborative partnerships to communicate the benefits and strategic importance of blended learning, thereby fostering a supportive ecosystem.

Through these targeted objectives, the project aims to not only address immediate challenges but also pave the way for long-term improvements and real changes in the educational landscape of Hong Kong.

2. The Infrastructure

Our project distinguishes itself through its innovative approaches to process and technology, grounded in the Complex Adaptive Blended Learning System (CABLS), as detailed in the Innovation Framework below. The framework presents a comprehensive ecosystem that encompasses all essential stakeholders in our project—Teacher, Learner, Institution, Content, Technology, and Learning Support.

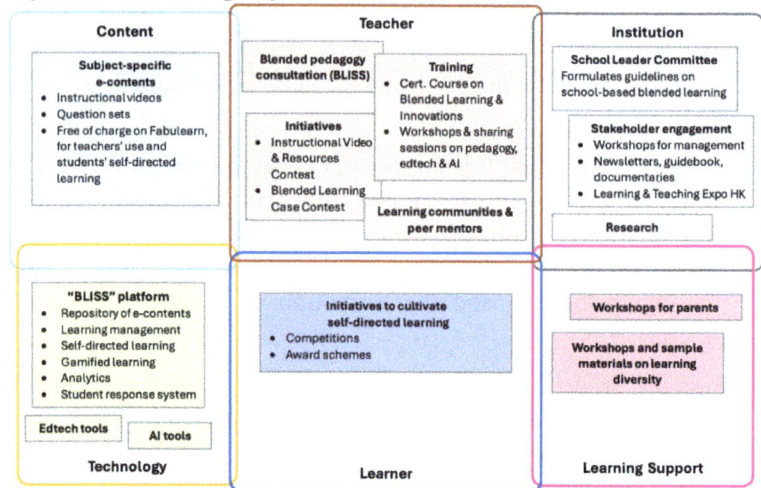

2.1 Teacher

To empower schools and frontline educators, our project has initiated the Blended Learning Innovations Support Scheme (BLISS), which is accessible to all primary and secondary teachers in Hong Kong. This robust program encompasses pedagogical consultation sessions and lesson study components. Our educational consultants work closely with teachers to co-design lessons, guiding them through the effective implementation of blended learning strategies. After the design phase, consultants observe classes and provide detailed, constructive feedback, helping teachers to critically evaluate and enhance their teaching methods.

The project provides numerous professional development opportunities for teachers, with a standout being our Peer-mentor Training Programme. Available to teachers engaged in BLISS, this initiative aims to empower experienced educators with the essential skills to support their colleagues, thereby enhancing collaborative learning environments and cultivating essential leadership skills for driving innovative teaching methods. The 25-hour program includes an exploration of the theoretical underpinnings of blended learning, practical applications customized for different subjects, a hands-on practicum, and enrichment activities. These activities feature online seminars and workshops focused on the integration and application of Generative AI tools, providing a dynamic and forward-thinking approach to education.

In addition, the project establishes a vibrant community of practice (CoP) that unites educational consultants from higher education, school leaders (e.g., principals and curriculum developers), and in-service primary and secondary teachers across four key learning areas: Chinese Language, English Language, Mathematics, and Science Education. This community is actively engaged and continually strengthened through a diverse array of enrichment activities, including workshops, seminars, sharing sessions, blended learning case contests, and overseas exchange tours. We ensure that this partnership is not a one-way flow of activities from the university to K-12 schools. Through annual conferences and seminars, we foster the exchange of ideas and practices between K-12 and higher education, leading to innovative teaching methods and the adoption of best practices that benefit both educational levels. By promoting joint research initiatives, K-12 teachers and higher education researchers are given opportunities to collaborate on educational studies, share findings, and implement evidence-based practices, ultimately enhancing the overall educational landscape.

Figure 1: Annual conference that brought the CoP members from higher education and K-12 education together to share good practices of blended learning

2.2 Content

Many teachers recognize the advantages of blended learning, yet they often encounter significant challenges. The primary hurdle is the lack of time to create or source suitable high-quality online resources. Additionally, finding a platform that effectively monitors student learning presents another significant challenge. A common issue teachers report is students' failure to complete pre-class learning tasks, which undermines the effectiveness of in-class activities designed to build upon that preliminary learning.

To address these challenges and support teachers in implementing blended learning, we have developed a free digital platform called The BLISS Self-Learning Platform. This platform offers an extensive collection of teaching and learning resources, featuring over 1,000 instructional videos and exercises across subjects such as English, Chinese, Mathematics, and Science, catering to both primary and secondary education levels. Our goal is to expand this repository to 1,600 videos. This resource enables teachers to seamlessly incorporate high-quality educational content into their flipped lesson plans, greatly reducing the time and effort needed to create teaching materials from scratch.

2.3 Technology

Teachers also need practical advice on how to use technology in blended learning effectively. Recently, generative artificial intelligence (Gen-AI) in education has been gaining traction as a transformative tool that can simulate complex problem-solving scenarios, offer real-time feedback, and enhance personalized learning experiences. However, the integration of generative AI also introduces significant challenges that educators and students must navigate, particularly regarding ethical and responsible use.

Acknowledging the transformative potential of Gen-AI in blended learning, we have launched an initiative to educate teachers, students, and parents about Gen-AI and to provide them with the necessary skills. Our goal is to empower them to leverage Gen-AI in enhancing educational processes and student learning outcomes. Since 2023, we have hosted 15 workshops and events focused on incorporating Gen-AI into educational settings, attracting 1,950 participants, including educators, students, and parents. These sessions have spanned a broad spectrum of themes. For educators, we have explored the application of Gen-AI across various disciplines, such as Chinese writing and science education. Additionally, events like "Re-exploring Assessment Methods in the AI Era" have examined how assessment strategies need to evolve in response to the advent of Gen-AI. For students and parents, we have facilitated discussions on AI-enhanced creative storytelling and autonomous learning. These varied workshops underscore our dedication to equipping the educational community for the AI-enhanced future, establishing our role as a leader in educational innovation.

2.4 Learner

The BLISS Self-Learning Platform serves not only as a repository of teaching and learning resources for teachers but also as a digital platform designed to foster self-directed learning among students. It features various interactive elements aimed at boosting students' learning motivation and monitoring their progress. Each instructional video is paired with a set of questions that encourage students to self-assess their understanding and address any misconceptions. Additionally, videos are organized into "learning packages" by topic, offering a comprehensive understanding of each study area.

To further engage students and promote consistent use, the platform incorporates game-like elements. Students can earn badges for achieving learning goals or completing platform-defined challenges. They can also create their own learning challenges and invite peers to join, fostering a collaborative learning environment.

2.5 Institution

Adopting a new teaching approach involves more than just the dedication and expertise of teachers; it necessitates a collaborative effort to achieve meaningful change. It requires the support of school management, including the formulation of relevant policies, setting of instructional goals and directions, provision of adequate resources and training, staff allocation, and upgrading of in-school teaching equipment, etc.

Recognizing the crucial role of support from school leadership, a committee of school leaders has been established to develop and advocate for management strategies that align with the Framework of Complex Adaptive Blended Learning Systems (CABLS) (Wang, Han, and Yang, 2016). These strategies are centered on the six interactive key elements of CABLS: learner, teacher, content, institution, technology, and learning support. With this committee's backing, "A Guide to Blended Learning Implementation for School Leaders" (https://en.jcblendedlearning.hk/post/202409-guide-1) was compiled and distributed across all schools in Hong Kong. The Guide aims to offer foundational principles and actionable recommendations, such as staffing strategies, motivation enhancement techniques, and e-learning support, to assist school leaders who are committed to implementing blended learning on a broader scale.

2.6 Learning support

To provide adequate support for their children as they undertake self-learning tasks at home, parents should also grasp the fundamentals of blended learning.

Acknowledging the critical influence of parental involvement on students' educational outcomes, we launched a series of workshops tailored specifically for parents. These sessions aim to enhance their engagement in their children's blended learning process. Focused particularly on cutting-edge tools such as generative AI and learning analytics, the workshops are designed to improve parents' AI literacy, ensuring they possess the necessary knowledge and perspectives to effectively support their children's learning experiences in the 21st century.

Figure 2: In the workshop designed for parents and their children, various AI-based tools were introduced. Together, they collaborated to create a story using AI-generated texts and images.

3. The Challenges

The primary strategy of this project to enhance learning is the implementation of lesson study, a professional development process where groups of teachers and educational consultants collaboratively plan, observe, and analyze learning and teaching through "research lessons". While the Education Bureau (EDB) of Hong Kong has actively promoted the adoption of lesson study through various programs, some teachers remain skeptical about its effectiveness and are reluctant to participate.

Fostering a culture of collaboration among teachers and sustaining the impact of lesson study presents several challenges. Zhang (2015) identified major hindrances, including pressures from an examination-focused system, substantial workloads, parental expectations, and a lack of support and trust among staff members. Additionally, implementing lesson study requires a significant investment of time and resources. Schools need to allocate sufficient time for teachers to plan, observe, and reflect on lessons. Continuous support from school leadership and ongoing professional development are crucial to maintaining momentum and ensuring the long-term success of lesson study.

We adopted three approaches to mitigate the challenges associated with lesson study. First, we raise awareness and understanding of lesson study by sharing success stories from other schools and conducting demonstration lessons. We organize model lesson studies led by experienced teachers or educational consultants, showcasing the process and its positive outcomes. Secondly, we seek support from school leadership through "A Guide to Blended Learning Implementation for School Leaders," encouraging school leaders to actively support lesson study by providing necessary resources, such as time for planning and collaboration. Finally, we offer training for middle-level teachers, preparing them to become "peer mentors" equipped to facilitate co-planning lesson sessions independently. This peer mentoring system, where experienced teachers guide and support their colleagues through the lesson study process, fosters sustainable collaborative learning and teaching innovations.

4. How the Initiative Was Received

As of August 2024, the project has achieved significant milestones:

- Provided support to 420 teachers across 71 schools via BLISS, positively impacting over 9,200 students.
- Enabled 125 teachers to complete the Certificate Course, who now serve as peer mentors.
- Hosted 70 workshops on blended pedagogies and educational technology, attended by over 4,500 educators.
- Conducted 4 specialized workshops for 800 parents, equipping them with skills to support their children's blended learning.
- Attracted 1,100 visitors to our booth at LTExpo 2023.
- Registered over 18,000 students and 2,800 teachers on the Fabulearn platform (as of May 2024), providing access to more than 900 instructional resources.

e-Learning Excellence Awards
- Engaged over 3,500 students from 130+ schools in various competitions and award schemes.

The participation in our events was notably high, with active sharing of experiences by teachers, underscoring our significant impact. A 16-member School Leader Committee was also established to formulate guidelines for innovative teaching methods, demonstrating a strong commitment to implementing blended learning at the institutional level.

The effectiveness of our project is profound, as supported by the feedback collected from our first-year engagement surveys and interviews with teachers and students from partner schools, along with participants from our training events, to assess their perceptions of blended learning and gain insights into how these perceptions evolved over the course of the project. A resounding 83% of teachers confirmed their understanding of blended learning has significantly enhanced, while 80% reported an increased level of confidence in implementing blended learning strategies. Our project's influence extends to students as well, with 72% of primary school students and 59% of secondary school students attesting to an enhanced ability for self-directed learning, a key benefit of the blended learning approach. At our events designed for teachers, an average of 87% of participants reported a boost in their confidence and knowledge pertaining to effective blended learning strategies.

In addition, our self-learning platform has been the cornerstone of our impact. Currently, the platform is a go-to platform for students who previously had limited access to quality digital resources. Since its launch, more than 16,000 students from all backgrounds have been actively using the platform for their learning needs. We surveyed over 700 primary and secondary schools who have access to the platform and the feedback was overwhelmingly positive:

- About 65% reported an increase in their capabilities and motivation for self-learning.
- Over 70% felt that they now had more resources and support for self-learning
- Nearly 70% found that the resources on the platform to be useful

Lastly, our parent engagement workshops have had an inspiring impact on disadvantaged students' learning journeys. These workshops have equipped nearly 800 parents with the knowledge and skills to support their children's learning in a blended environment. The workshops have resulted in increased home-based involvement in children's education, fostering a supportive home learning environment that is critical for the success of disadvantaged students. Survey responses gathered from parents affirmed the effectiveness of the workshops. Over 90% indicated that the workshops met their needs well, and they would recommend them to other parents for future sessions.

5. The Learning Outcomes

We conducted a study to assess the impact of blended learning on self-regulated learning and motivation among primary and secondary students in Hong Kong. The study involved 249 students—159 from five secondary schools and 90 from five primary schools—who were instructed by teachers engaged in a professional development program associated with this project. We employed a modified version of Pintrich et al.'s (1990) "Motivated Strategies for Learning Questionnaire" (MSLQ) to track changes in the students' self-regulation and motivation at the beginning and end of the 2022/23 academic year. Using a paired samples t-test for our analysis, we noted significant enhancements in "self-regulated strategies" among the primary school group, and improvements in both "self-regulated strategies" and "self-efficacy beliefs" in the secondary school group. However, there was no significant change in "intrinsic" or "extrinsic motivation" for either group. These results indicate that while blended learning can improve certain cognitive and metacognitive skills, its effect on motivational constructs might take longer to emerge. The varied responses between primary and secondary students suggest that developmental stages may influence the effectiveness of blended learning. This highlights the need for instructional designs that are tailored to the developmental needs of different age groups.

Empowered by this project, teachers have also significantly bolstered these positive developments, fostering a supportive educational environment that motivates and uplifts students. The following videos highlight the concrete outcomes of this initiative:

Video highlighting the project achievements in the first project year:	 https://youtu.be/nzU6WukLSZg

Video showing the perspectives from one of our partner schools:	 https://youtu.be/5atIOGLTQGU

6. Plans to Further Develop the Initiative

Over the next few years, we aim to significantly expand and enrich both the use and capabilities of our BLISS Self-Learning Platform and our exploration of Gen-AI in Hong Kong's secondary and primary school sectors. Our goal is to transform the platform into a go-to tool for blended learning in Chinese-speaking regions that is comparable to Khan Academy and Junyi Academy. We are currently enhancing the platform by incorporating more interactive features (such as inviting learning buddies and sending a "challenge" to their peers) and broadening the range of resources across different subjects. Concurrently, we will concentrate on enhancing AI and IT literacy among teachers and students, equipping them for a future where education is increasingly influenced by technology. We will delve into the use of generative AI in Hong Kong's schools, gathering and disseminating best practices through articles and learning circles to motivate educators.

References

Moorhouse, B. L. (2021) 'Beginning teaching during Covid-19: Newly qualified Hong Kong teachers' preparedness for online teaching', *Educational Studies*, pp.1–17. Available at: https://doi.org/10.1080/03055698.2021.1964939

Pintrich, P. R., and de Groot, E. V. (1990) 'Motivational and self-regulated learning components of classroom academic performance', *Journal of Educational Psychology*, 82(1), pp. 33–40. https://doi.org/10.1037/0022-0663.82.1.33

Sharma, M. (2019) 'The changing role of teacher in blended learning', *International Journal of Applied Research* , 5(8), pp. 325–327.

Wang, Y., Han, X. and Yang, J. (2015) 'Revisiting the blended learning literature: Using a complex adaptive systems framework', *Journal of Educational Technology & Society*, 18(2), pp. 380–393. Available at: https://www.j-ets.net/ETS/journals/18_2/28.pdf

Yeung, M. W. and Yau, A. H. (2021) 'A thematic analysis of higher education students' perceptions of online learning in Hong Kong under covid-19: Challenges, strategies and support', *Education and Information Technologies*. Available at: https://doi.org/10.1007/s10639-021-10656-3

Zhang, Y. E. (2016) 'Sustaining lesson study in Hong Kong primary schools with leadership for learning', Paper presented at the 2016 AERA Annual Meeting: Public scholarship to educate diverse democracies, The Walter E. Washington Convention Centre, Washington, DC.

Author Biographies

Professor Paul Lam is the Associate Director at the Centre for eLearning Innovation and Technology (ELITE) at The Chinese University of Hong Kong. He specializes in teaching and learning principles, web-assisted education, and the evaluation of eLearning and mLearning. He has also designed educational tools, including uReply, a classroom student response system developed under his supervision.

Carmen Lau serves as Project Manager at the Centre for Learning Enhancement and Research (CLEAR) at The Chinese University of Hong Kong. She has managed multiple e-learning projects at university and school levels, fostering communities of practice among teachers to drive teaching innovation.

Man Tsang serves as Assistant Project Manager at the Centre for Learning Enhancement And Research (CLEAR) at The Chinese University of Hong Kong. She has been working in initiatives at both the university level and in primary and secondary schools with an aim to enhance the learning experience and improve student outcomes across various educational settings.

BP4WE: Best Practices for Workgroup E-assessment with WebAVALIA

Rosalina Babo
CEOS.PP, ISCAP, Polytechnic of Porto, Portugal
babo@iscap.ipp.pt

Abstract: Problem-based learning (PBL) projects have gained prominence as a means for students to develop essential skills and competencies. Whenever these projects are developed in group, these provide opportunities to enhance teamwork and other critical skills. However, assessing individual contributions within workgroups poses challenges, as not all members contribute equally or in the same manner. Ensuring fairness in grading becomes a significant concern for evaluators, and traditional methods often result in biased and unfair assessments. To address this issue, self and peer assessment practices have emerged as a solution. By allowing students to express their opinions on their own work and their peers' contributions, these assessment methods provide a more comprehensive and unbiased assessment. WebAVALIA, a self and peer e-assessment software, has been developed to support evaluators in distinguishing individual contributions within workgroups. This user-friendly tool provides an easy, quick, and anonymous assessment process. WebAVALIA uses workgroup members' perceptions of their own and their peers' performance and contributions, to deliver fair and unbiased assessments. This case history involves students of information technologies, where WebAVALIA was employed to assess them throughout a PBL project. The software ensured that individual contributions were acknowledged within the workgroup. This case demonstrates the effectiveness of WebAVALIA in promoting fair assessments and allowing the students a sense of recognition for their contribution.WebAVALIA provides a practical solution to the assessment challenges faced in workgroup projects. By using this software, evaluators can accurately evaluate individual performance and foster fairness. The integration of WebAVALIA into educational initiatives empowers students to develop essential skills while experiencing a more unbiased and rewarding learning environment.

1. Introduction

In today's digital age, students of Information Technologies (IT) need to complement the learning of theoretical topics with practical topics, where the know-how is expected as a learning outcome. Along with develop a range of skills to keep up with the fast-paced technology landscape. These skills include problem-solving, process, and content skills, critical thinking, as well as soft skills, namely communication, cooperation, leadership, autonomy, and presentation skills (Alias et al., 2015; Ananiadou & Claro, 2009; Babo &

e-Learning Excellence Awards
Suhonen, 2018; Babo et al., 2020; Frank & Barzilai, 2004; Khoiriyah & Husamah, 2018; Loyens et al., 2015; Stevens & Norman, 2016; Tiwari et al., 2017).

Problem-based learning (PBL) is an instruction approach that can help the students to consolidate the knowledge learned throughout the semester, as well as develop and improve skills and competencies. The purpose of PBL is to provide students with a guided learning experience in learning by presenting them with a real-life problem. They are required to apply their previous acquired knowledge, to accomplish tasks and identify the best solution to the problem, thus supporting the theoretical learning outcomes and promoting the development of problem-solving skills (Babo et al., 2020; Hmelo-Silver, 2004; Khoiriyah & Husamah, 2018; Loyens et al., 2015; Savery, 2015).

Another feature possible in PBL it the use of small workgroups where the students have to participate in discussions and arguments. Through these interactions, the students have to apply their acquired knowledge to solve the presented problem, which leads them to engage in their own learning experience. The implementation of a workgroups is an added value to assist the students in developing skills and competencies (Hmelo-Silver, 2004; Loyens *et al.*, 2015; Khoiriyah and Husamah, 2018; Rienties and Tempelaar, 2018).

However, literature states a students' lack of interest in working in groups which derives from several aspects, one being that when working in group there is the possible unfairness in individual assessment. This can happen because some members are less committed than others, which leads to different contribution rates, but not always compatible assessments. A mark in the students' academic life is important for their success and sense of reward, and providing distinctions in the workgroup can motivating them to work harder (Babo et al., 2020; Babo, 2021; Daba et al., 2017).

Nonetheless, the task of "performing a fair and accurate assessment of individual student contributions to the work produced by a team as well as assessing teamwork itself presents numerous challenges", as not all members contribute equally or in the same manner. Therefore, ensuring fairness in grading becomes a significant concern for evaluators, and traditional methods often result in biased and unfair assessments. Usually, the evaluators would attribute the same mark to the whole workgroup which not always corresponds to the actual contribution and performance of each individual (Babo et al., 2021; Clark et al., 2005).

One way to surpass this is to use self and peer assessment practices. By allowing students to express their opinions on their own work and their peers' contributions, these assessment methods provide a more comprehensive and unbiased assessment. It is a great strategy for the students to contribute to others' work, because they are not only evaluating themselves, but are also evaluating the rest of the workgroup, and thus engage them in group learning as well.

This case history describes how the usage of PBL by the Information Systems (IS) Department, at Porto Accounting and Business School (ISCAP), address this issue. The increased use of PBL at ISCAP, led the teachers to decide to also increase the weight of these workgroup projects in the students' final assessment. Thus, to ensure that the students were distinguished by their performance in a workgroup, self and peer assessment practices were the method (Babo & Suhonen, 2018; Babo et al., 2020, 2021).

2. Workgroup assessment challenges

At a first instance, the challenge was the great number of students per class. The IS Department at ISCAP is composed of about twenty teachers who teach all degree programs. Each teacher can have approximately 150 students in a semester, which can lead to 30 to 40 workgroups per semester, considering groups are ideally composed of 3 to 4 members. Thus, the teacher might not have an objective perception of the most working students in a workgroup when most of the work development is done outside the classroom. Even if there were continuous contact with the workgroups during all the development process, without a rigorous observation method, the teacher would still not achieve a real perception on the actual performance of each workgroup member.

One main concern with workgroups is the assessment process, which should be an active part of the learning process with emphasis on self- and peer assessment. Since the grades are given individually, that is, each student within a workgroup will achieve an individual grade, the evaluators are often taken back with the challenging task of providing fair and unbiased marks. Teachers often feel that workgroup assessment leads to "anxiety, guilt, and uncertainty", and that the assessment can be performed in an "imprecise and unsystematic" way (Forsell, Forslund Frykedal and Chiriac, 2021, p. 2).

Some of the challenges described in literature are the difficulty in distinguish individual's performance, lack of an objective perception about the students who work the most in a workgroup, lack of a rigorous observation method to achieve a real insight on the actual performance of each member, and ultimately the unfairness and biased final grades. With the use of self and peer assessment practices in these classes, teachers were able to achieve a more reliable way to guarantee that everyone would be assessed according to their performance.

However, considering the number of students being assessed, these practices can add to teachers' already limited time and work, increasing their administrative tasks. Furthermore, the teachers needed to find a solution to alleviate the assessment management and increased workload from these tasks, so that the teaching activities would not be impacted.

To overcome this challenge, the teachers of the IS Department, at ISCAP, searched for ways to ease the self and peer assessment task, while ensure the continuity of the teaching activities. The solution found was to use e-assessment to support the assessment management, which can assist the teachers in their laborious, time-consuming, and complex task of distinguish members in workgroups.

3. WebAVALIA initiative

WebAVALIA was built within ISCAP's environment and involved its staff and facilities. The knowledge base for the framework development consisted of theoretical topics about the assessment process, such as PBL, self and peer assessment, workgroup assignments, knowledge of coding technology, as well as other e-assessment software tools offered in the market. Also, the expertise of the senior lectures was an important aspect (Babo et al., 2020).

The first version of the software was called "AVALIA" and was implemented in 2012. Since then, several versions were implemented, and the perception of fairness and assessment accuracy of the tool has changed through the years. In 2014, a web version of the software - WebAVALIA - was developed and it has been improved to support evaluators in distinguishing individual contributions within workgroups. It aims to assist the teacher with the task of distinguishing the elements of a workgroup by supporting the students' self and peer assessment. The software ensured that individual contributions were acknowledged within the workgroup.

WebAVALIA is a self and peer e-assessment software designed to assist evaluators in distinguishing individual contributions to workgroups, providing an easy, quick, anonymous, and fair assessment. It uses the perceptions of the workgroup members of their own and their peers' performance, and contributions to the project's development to provide a fair and unbiased assessment that considers the overall project grade. This allows for a sense of fairness and reward among students, which can lead to greater openness and willingness towards collaborative work.

It aims to provide a practical solution to the assessment challenges faced in workgroup projects. With this software, evaluators can accurately assess individual performance and foster fairness. The integration of WebAVALIA into educational initiatives empowers students to develop essential skills while experiencing a more unbiased and rewarding learning environment. WebAVALIA is available to other institutions that intend to use it, by contacting the tool administrator.

Considering that the main users of WebAVALIA are the students, to gather how this initiative was received, the students' opinions and perceptions were collected through the distribution of surveys, along the years. These were composed by five-point Likert scales, and open-answer questions where students were asked about the advantages and disadvantages of using this tool, and comments and suggestions. The resulting data analysis cannot be fully presented in this paper, since the analysis covers more than 400 students. In the foreseeable future, there will be the presentation of the results.

Nonetheless, the first analysis of the results indicates that the developed method provides fairness in the assessment of workgroup members, delivering a distinction amongst individuals. Therefore, each member obtains a mark that corresponds to their specific contribution to the workgroup. Table 1 displays some advantages expressed by the students in the survey's open-ended questions.

Table 1: WebAVALIA advantages mentioned by the students

S	Students' opinions
S2	"It allows for greater fairness in the work each member contributed to the final project. The grade for each group member is fairer."
S15	"It enables the assessment to be as accurate and fair as possible because when students run the application individually, they have an ease that they wouldn't have in other circumstances to express their opinion about the other group members. This will only generate unbiased and truthful opinions and, on the other hand, serve as motivation for everyone to work on the project, as there is always the idea that they will be assessed individually and not "dragged" along with others."
S56	"It is a more efficient and simple assessment method that allows the teacher to better understand the level of participation in the work by each group member."
S57	"It was a good initiative to create this tool, and it should suggest it for other courses."
S77	"Fast, simple, fair; it involves students in the assessment of their own work."

The students' feedback allows us to infer that WebAVALIA is a valuable asset as an assessment tool for workgroups. It enables differentiation based on the students' performance in project development. It also allows the teacher to gain a better understanding of the work carried out by the group members. The users considered that this e-assessment initiative has a positive influence on the workgroups' productivity, being a fair and simple tool.

The first analysis of the results indicates that the developed method provides fairness in the assessment of group members, delivering a distinction amongst individuals. Therefore, each group member obtains a mark that corresponds to their specific contribution to the workgroup. WebAVALIA helped the students gain the feeling that the assessment was fair and that their efforts had been adequately rewarded when working in groups. In turn, it helped them feel that it is possible to achieve fair and unbiased assessments of workgroups, understand its usefulness and consider it indispensable.

4. Best practices for workgroups e-assessment

To assist students in achieving learning goals and attaining important skills and competencies, teachers can implement workgroup projects. However, to promote fair assessment and allow the students a sense of recognition for their contribution to the workgroup, it is essential to follow some practices. Here is a list of best practices for workgroup e-assessment:

1. IT students need to have the know how to accomplish tasks and apply knowledge, as well as develop a certain range of skills. In order to assist the teachers with the assessment related to the skill and competency acquisition, they can use PBL approaches, namely workgroups. Workgroups provide students with opportunities to collaborate and engage in their own learning;

2. During the assessment of students in workgroups, their active participation and contributions throughout the project's development should be considered. The group assessment criteria must include several aspects, namely the learning process, the final product quality, its report and presentation;

3. The task of distinguishing workgroup members can be performed with the implementation of self and peer assessment practices. This method encourages students to reflect on their own performance and provide feedback to their peers. By involving students in the assessment process,

a more comprehensive view of their individual and workgroup achievements can be achieved.

4. To assist in this complex task, teachers can make use of WebAVALIA, to guarantee a more unbiased and rewarding learning environment, ensuring that the individual contributions are acknowledged within the workgroup. This e-assessment tool offers features that promote more accurate assessments of individual contributions within the workgroup. With WebAVALIA, teachers can provide students with an unbiased assessment experience and ensure that their efforts and achievements are recognized and rewarded.

5. Future of the initiative

In the future, it is expected to continue the improvement of WebAVALIA. The improvement of the platform is directly related to user experience and usability thus it is planned to present of results from the data analysis.

It would be important to understand the tool's generalization, by comprehending how other universities, technical training students, and cultures or countries experience this tool.

There are plans to implement the method in other workgroup assessment contexts – such as sports and business environments, other higher education institutions, technical training students – in other cultures and countries. From this myriad of contexts, satisfaction results would be compared.

Acknowledgments

This work is financed by Portuguese national funds through FCT - Fundação para a Ciência e Tecnologia, under the project UIDB/05422/2020.

References

Alias, M., Masek, A. and Salleh, H.H.M. (2015) 'Self, peer and teacher assessments in problem based learning: Are they in agreements?', *Procedia - Social and Behavioral Sciences*, 204, pp. 309–317. Available at: https://doi.org/10.1016/J.SBSPRO.2015.08.157.

Ananiadou, K. and Claro, M. (2009) '21st century skills and competences for new millennium learners in OECD countries', *OECD Education Working Papers*, 41. Available at: http://repositorio.minedu.gob.pe/handle/123456789/2529 (Accessed: 27 November 2018).

Babo, R. (2021) *Improving individual and collaborative E-assessment through multiple-choice questions and WebAVALIA: A new e-assessment strategy implemented at a Portuguese university*. University of Eastern Finland.

Babo, R. *et al.* (2021) 'Self and Peer E-Assessment: A Study on Software Usability', https://services.igi-global.com/resolvedoi/resolve.aspx?doi=10.4018/IJICTE.20210701.oa5, 17(3), pp. 68–85. Available at: https://doi.org/10.4018/IJICTE.20210701.OA5.

Babo, R. and Suhonen, J. (2018) 'E-assessment with multiple choice questions: a qualitative study of teachers' opinions and experience regarding the new assessment strategy', *International Journal of Learning Technology*, 13(3), p. 220. Available at: https://doi.org/10.1504/IJLT.2018.095964.

Babo, R., Suhonen, J. and Tukiainen, M. (2020) 'Improving workgroup assessment with WebAVALIA: The concept, framework and first results', *Journal of Information Technology Education: Innovations in Practice*, 19, pp. 157–184. Available at: https://doi.org/10.28945/4627.

Clark, N., Davies, P. and Skeers, R. (2005) 'Self and peer assessment in software engineering projects', in *Proceedings of the 7th Australasian conference on Computing education - Volume 42*. Newcastle, pp. 91–100. Available at: https://dl.acm.org/doi/10.5555/1082424.1082436 (Accessed: 15 January 2019).

Daba, T.M., Ejersa, S.J. and Aliyi, S. (2017) 'Student perception on group work and group assignments in classroom teaching: The case of Bule Hora university second year biology students, South Ethiopia: An action research', *Educational Research and Reviews*, 12(17), pp. 860–866.

Forsell, J., Forslund Frykedal, K. and Chiriac, E.H. (2021) 'Teachers' perceived challenges in group work assessment', *http://www.editorialmanager.com/cogentedu*, 8(1). Available at: https://doi.org/10.1080/2331186X.2021.1886474.

Frank, M. and Barzilai, A. (2004) 'Integrating alternative assessment in a project-based learning course for pre-service science and technology teachers', *Assessment & Evaluation in Higher Education*, (1), pp. 41–61. Available at: https://doi.org/10.1080/0260293042000160401.

Hmelo-Silver, C.E. (2004) 'Problem-Based Learning: What and how do students learn?', *Educational Psychology Review*, 16(3), pp. 235–266. Available at: https://doi.org/10.1023/B:EDPR.0000034022.16470.f3.

Khoiriyah, A.J. and Husamah, H. (2018) 'Problem-based learning: Creative thinking skills, problem-solving skills, and learning outcome of seventh grade students', *Jurnal Pendidikan Biologi Indonesia*, 4(2), pp. 151–160. Available at: https://doi.org/10.22219/jpbi.v4i2.5804.

Loyens, S.M.M. et al. (2015) 'Problem-based learning as a facilitator of conceptual change', *Learning and Instruction*, 38, pp. 34–42. Available at: https://doi.org/10.1016/J.LEARNINSTRUC.2015.03.002.

Rienties, B. and Tempelaar, D. (2018) 'Turning Groups Inside Out: A Social Network Perspective', *Journal of the Learning Sciences*, 27(4), pp. 550–579. Available at: https://doi.org/10.1080/10508406.2017.1398652.

Savery, J.R. (2015) 'Overview of problem-based learning: Definitions and distinctions', in *Essential readings in problem-based learning: Exploring and extending the legacy of Howard S. Barrows*. Purdue University Press, pp. 5–15. Available at: https://books.google.pt/books?hl=en&lr=&id=KhF-BgAAQBAJ&oi=fnd&pg=PA5&ots=awlcmUjCTx&sig=Qlt03j2QEE2i0HAlQyhVEmMqXtA&dir_esc=y#v=onepage&q&f=false (Accessed: 1 February 2019).

Stevens, M. and Norman, R. (2016) 'Industry expectations of soft skills in IT graduates a regional survey', in *ACSW '16: Proceedings of the Australasian Computer Science Week Multiconference*. New York, NY, USA: ACM, pp. 1–9. Available at: https://doi.org/10.1145/2843043.2843068.

Tiwari, R., Arya, R.K. and Bansal, M. (2017) 'Motivating students for project-based learning for application of research methodology skills.', *International journal of applied & basic medical research*, 7, pp. S4–S7. Available at: https://doi.org/10.4103/ijabmr.IJABMR_123_17.

Author Biography

Rosalina Babo is a Coordinator Professor of Information Systems Department at ISCAP/P.Porto. Rosalina is the Director of SAP University Alliance at P.Porto. Among other functions she was Head of the IS Department (+20 years), member of the university scientific board (12 years), founder of CEOS.PP (former CEISE STI) research centre and its director (5 years).

Greencool Online and Blended Learning MOOC

[1]**Edit Kővári, [1]Anastasiia Turusinova and [2]Réka Vámosi**
[1]GreenCool project expert, University of Pannonia, Hungary
[2]University of Tartu, Estonia,
kovari.edit@gtk.uni-pannon.hu
anastasiia.turusinova@ut.ee
vamosi.reka@uni-pannon.hu

Abstract: GreenCool is an Erasmus+ project which was initiated by 4 European Capitals of Culture universities: University of Pannonia, Veszprém (HU), University of Tartu, Tartu (EST), Vytautas Magnus University, Kaunas (LT), West University of Timisoara, Timisoara (RO) and Militos Consulting S.A. (GR). The general goal is to develop environmental awareness among youth and to spread the thought of sustainable development among the widest possible age groups at events that attract large audience. We committed to develop an innovative online massive open online course (MOOC) and also an open platform accompanied by a pilot national and international blended curricula for higher education students. Furthermore, our goal is to equip students with communication tools and sustainable attitude to become effective advocates/green influencer for advancing EU green economy and culture. The course has a scientific base, as the partners did a thorough needs analyses first including quantitative research with nearly 800 students, and focus group interviews with educator, influencers and green experts. Based on the results a 5-module course was created, where each module has a knowledge, inspiration and action section. The *Knowledge* part introduces the given communication- presentation method and the main basics of the given green issue. In the *Inspiration* part there are examples (e.g. videos with a Z generation influencer whom we cooperated) combined with some exercises. While in the *Action* part participants have to do an action (creating art, Peach-Kucha, Forum etc.) by combining the learnt communication techniques with a green issue they choose. Learning outcomes of the course were measured through Bloom's taxonomy and aligned with knowledge, inspiration and action parts. The national blended (online course plus in-person teaching) pilot courses with more than 100 students took place in 2023 fall simultaneously in all 4 universities. While the international MOOC course has been hosted by University of Tartu in the 2024 spring semester with 200 students. Both end with green issue presentation by the students (verbal, artistic, flashmob etc.) at a European Capital of Culture (ECoC) event. You can learn more about the project here: https://greencoolproject.eu/en/home/ and the open platform in 6 languages (which will be finalized and available from 2024 autumn) here: https://training.greencoolproject.eu/, and follow the activities, students' projects on Facebook: https://www.facebook.com/greencoolproject.

e-Learning Excellence Awards

1. Introduction and objectives of GreenCool

When Veszprém and the University of Pannonia learnt the results to be European Capital of Culture (ECoC) in 2023 we grabbed the opportunity to prepare a proposal for the upcoming ECoC partner universities to create something special together. The concept was that all ECoC cities deal in one or another way with sustainability and green issues. But hardly any involve university students that can be 10% of the city population (even if they are just temporary) who can be influenced and who can influence themselves the peers and other generations. They communication channels are usually social media platforms, and the style is also different from everyday communication. Therefore, we approached those university partners who are specialized in green and/or communication research and practices to create a MOOC and blended course which can call the attention to the European youth toward Sustainable Development Goals. This is how our project *GreenCool-Let me influence your green self!* was born.

The overarching objective is twofold: first, to enhance environmental consciousness among university students, and second, to promote the principles of sustainable development across diverse age groups during high-attendance events. Our commitment involves creating innovative online course materials and integrating sustainable development concepts into all higher education curricula. Additionally, recognizing the persuasive influence of young advocates, we seek to engage audiences of all ages at cultural events and festivals held in various European Capitals of Culture. Our aim is to foster environmentally responsible behaviour and encourage active participation in sustainable development efforts. Furthermore, we aspire to equip students with effective communication tools and a sustainable mind-set, empowering them to advocate for the advancement of the EU's green economy and cultural initiatives. Our message is to teach as many people as possible to think greener, to believe in sustainable development not only in environmental, but also in the social, cultural and economic spheres.

We believe in the idea of "thinking local, acting globally' is the 21st century phenomenon, as during the project youth become opinion leaders/influencers who can blog an idea in their room in front of the computer and have a huge global effect in quick time! The place where we are living is not just about the environment but rather the way of life. Local values remain where you live. This approach is in harmony with the value of the ECoC as well. Innovation aspects in keywords: technological developments, green ambassadors, to try out of 21st-century influencer techniques offline, European Capitals of Culture values and challenges bond universities-towns-students-citizens.

2. The infrastructure

To develop an online course and educational materials we believed that a thorough background and needs analyses have to be carried out. Therefore, GreenCool Partnership reviewed hundreds articles, best practices and case studies, conducted a survey with more than 700 students, young adults and influencers, organised numerous focus-group interviews in the partner ECoC cities and developed the *Greenfluence Practice Collection and Research* (the full report is available on GreenCool website: https://greencoolproject.eu/en/project-results/).

The aim of the secondary and primary analyses was to gather information about youth knowledge and attitude on the two main issues: social media (both following and applying it) especially focusing on influencers and green-related topics. The analyses show when looking to the meaning of influencing, it could be noted, that often focus group participants do not consider themselves as influencers, "meaning a person who creates quality content and who has to convey entertainment to those who follow them". But on the other hand, it is interesting to note, that there are some participants who believe that "we are all influencers in some way" or who mentioned that "influencer is not only online, but you can also see an offline influencer". When discussing communication channels and techniques, it could be noted that all group participants are active sharing their ideas and experiences in various platforms such as: Tik Tok, Instagram, YouTube, Facebook, WhatsApp, LinkedIn, etc., and that "platforms are changing by time to time". Regarding the content, participants of all groups share their ideas about visual content as well as the content using various storytelling tools and inspirations, noticing that: "people really like simplicity and authenticity". The credibility of an influencer is gained by exemplary behavior and charity deed that is in connection with social issue. Youth follow both local and international influencers (language is not a barrier as 96.5% of the respondents speaks good English) and they follow local but also internationally well-known influencers. Those who already considered themselves influencers want to improve their content and storytelling script video writing skills. According to the questionnaire however influencers and politicians are less trusted in general among these youth. Parents and experts by 90% are the most trusted followed by teachers and friends. Regarding green and environmental issues experts and teachers are the most trusted, followed by a friend and NGOs, and the least trusted are the public institutions. Youth stop following influencers mostly when they get bored of them; or when they are not producing quality content; or no longer represent the issue they started with or post too many advertisements. Two thirds of the respondents in the questionnaire follow influencers who post environmental issues and half of them share news related to environmental topics. This means that youth are interested both in theory and in action considering green issues.

Based on the research outcomes, the following 12 communication techniques/methods/means and 12 green issues were suggested to be included in the ECoC Greenfluencer course:

- Communication techniques and structure of discourse: Storytelling on and offline; Blogging/glossary writing; Short film, video (You Tube, TikTok); Instagram, TikTok techniques offline-acting; How to create powerful picture content; Elevator pitch; Pecha Kucha; Oxford debate; TED talk; Gamification; Creative and circular communication; Round-table discussion.

- Green topics: Nutrition and food-waste; Sustainable fashion; Urban lifestyles, sustainable public living; Responsible consumption: small household habits, individual's responsibility; Energy saving and alternative energy: air and water quality and quantity; Collective social responsibility: individuals, companies and institutions; Critical recycling techniques, waste management and circular economy; Climate-phobia and anxiety; Greenwashing and ethical thinking; Green mobility.

Out of these results the following five Modules were created that mixed green and communication issues. Module 1 is about the introduction to soil biodiversity and circular and creative communication with symbols. Module 2 covers the key concepts and fundamentals of the following communication and speech delivery techniques: blogging, elevator pitch, Pecha Kucha, Oxford debate and TEDx talk and also the essential elements of the following green issues: zero waste, food waste, bioeconomy, precision economy and circular economy. Module 3 focuses on digital video crafting on social responsibility and responsible consumption. Module 4 is about sustainable living, fashion and the way you craft your story by persuasion. Module 5 is on creative communication by arts and smart mobility.

Module I: Introduction to green and communication basics: soil biodiversity and circular and creative communication with symbols

Module 1.1 There is no planet B

Module 1.2 Soil biodiversity

Module 1.3 Communication, circular communication and creativity

Edit Kővári, Anastasiia Turusinova and Réka Vámosi

Module 1.4 The role of symbols: from religious symbols to emojis

Module II: craft your green story

Module 2.1 Blogging – how to reduce food waste?

Module 2.2 Elevator pitch – zero waste family

Module 2.3 Pecha kucha – bioeconomy, precision economy

Module 2.4 Oxford debate – circular economy

Module 2.5 TEDx – How does generation z think about sustainability?

Module III: digital video crafting on social responsibility and responsible consumption

Module 3.1 Collective social responsibility

Module 3.2 Digital video crafting

Module IV: Crafting your story's ethical arguments

Module 4.1 Sustainable living and greenwashing

Module 4.2 What is persuasion?

Module V: Creative communication by arts through renewable energy and smart mobility

Module 5.1. Communication by arts

Module 5.2. A picture is worth a thousand words

Module 5.3. Installations, exhibitions, artistic demonstrations and actions

Module 5.4. Art in motion and action: music, flashmob, drama performances

The course material was developed in a systematic logic to divide each module to *Knowledge, Inspiration, Action* parts. In The *Knowledge* part there is a short introduction to the given green and communication topics. In *the Inspiration* part learners see examples (e.g. video, case study), while in the *Action* part learners can practice by combining the learnt communication techniques with the green issues. There are interactive and self-check activities in the Inspiration and Action part. Also, in some Modules an internal Forum (opinion board) is created for those who take the course to interact with each other. In each Module participants are offered a wide range of activities that they could interact with. (Picture 1).

The course was developed on University of Tartu Moodle platform that provides a lot of flexibility to the organisation of study materials. The other university partners adopted, translated and adjusted the English version to their own Moodle system.

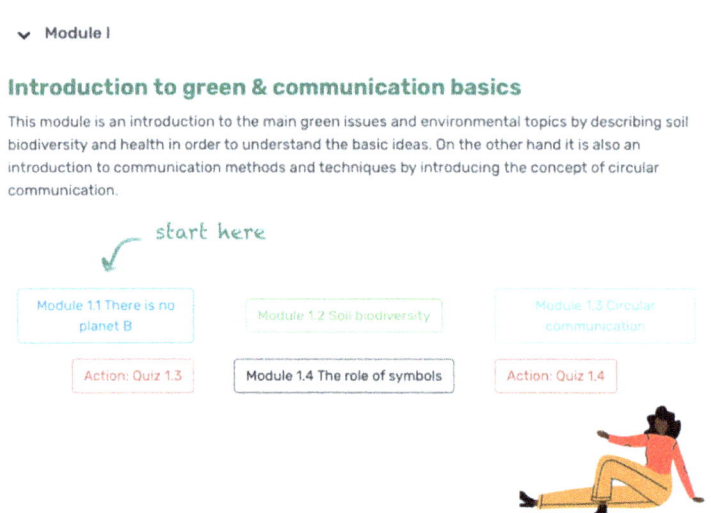

Figure 1: Example of the course structure (Module 1).

Course participants were able to track their study progress through "Completion progress" bar. This tool indicated which activities are overdue (red colour) which ones are yet to be completed (blue colour) and which ones are successfully completed (green), (Picture 2).

Figure 2: Example of completion progress bar.

Edit Kővári, Anastasiia Turusinova and Réka Vámosi

In the summer of 2023, the MOOC and educational materials for in-person teaching were tested by students at a summer camp on the Lake Balaton in Hungary. There were 2 lectures/experts from each university and 1 evaluation expert from Militos (altogether 9), and 2 students/influencers from each university (altogether 8). During the 5-day training the lecturers, experts, influencers and university students worked both in mixed and separate groups/pairs or individually to decide the best way to finalize and try out the MOOC material (on the basis 1 day 1 Module). Through training, we help volunteer university students/influencers how to shape the attitudes of communities towards sustainable development. Feedback was also collected from both students and trainers through on-site observers at the end of each module, as well as through an online QA questionnaire at the end of the entire workshop. The main idea was to find out if the material was feasible for them. This valuable feedback allowed us to fine-tune the course before we proceeded with the pilots. In the fall of 2023, the blended courses were launched at the four partners' universities in their national languages. More than 100 students were involved. During the autumn semester the course was managed and mentored by a main lecturer with invited co-lecturers. Student completed the MOOC piloting and had individual, pair and group work according to the syllabus mentored and facilitated by the main lecturer. Students gained university credits after completing the course.

The outcome of the blended ECoC Greenfluencer pilot course was a participation at an ECoC event/festival in November-December 2023, where students tried and tested their knowledge and influence audience offline in each ECoC cities. In Tartu three diverse organizations were selected for the event, offering participants a journey-like experience. The first stop, Paranduskelder, focuses on repair and upcycling activities to instigate changes in habits and mindsets. At Tartu Environmental Education Centre, participants engaged in educational activities and provided feedback on exhibitions addressing climate change. The final destination, A. Le Coq, showcased sustainable practices in manufacturing and marketing. With 29 participants from varied backgrounds, including students from different Estonian schools, the event received positive feedback, reflecting a shared belief in the importance of youth in shaping a sustainable future. In Timisoara students were encouraged to create short Instagram videos showcasing cultural events across Timisoara and Timis County, listed on the official agenda of Timisoara European Capital of Culture. Communication materials were subsequently shared on the dedicated Instagram page "Student eco in Timisoara," which quickly amassed 116 followers and over 30,000 views. 55 participants took

e-Learning Excellence Awards

part in the GreenCool event. In Kaunas they organized walking lectures to engage with Land Art and a community event. Greenfluencer students documented their reflections on Land Art pieces encountered during the walking lectures, with examples displayed in an exhibition. In Veszprém the GreenCool event featured engaging presentations and artistic installations on various environmental topics by Greenfluencer students, fostering meaningful discussions among more than 50 attendees of all ages. Notably, there was an insightful discussion with the creators of the documentary "There is no Planet B," which is part of the MOOC material. The event also included student presentations and displays, followed by networking sessions and a screening of the documentary, culminating in a roundtable discussion. The innovation of these blended courses was how green can be communicated in diverse channels let it be art, social media, local factory etc.

The second part was the international MOOC offered by University of Tartu in 2024 spring semester which was warmly accepted by the students. We had 200 participants from 18 different countries that decided to take part in the course. Higher number of participants allowed to test the technical side of the course on Moodle. Even though many assignments were automated and designed in a way to be checked by Moodle itself, some of the assignments needed manual grading (it concerns most of the creative assignments e.g. video assignments, forum posts etc.) (Picture 3). However, timeframe of the MOOC allowed to handle the traffic, as it lasted eight weeks in total.

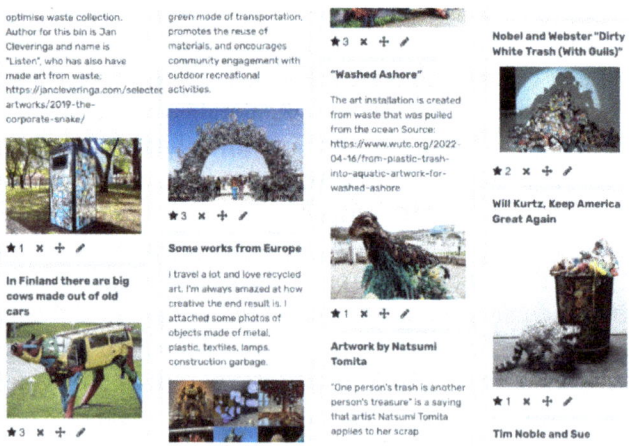

Figure 3: Trash art gallery as part of assignment Inspiration: Gallery 5.3.

The course will also be available on an open platform from 2024 September to the public. The aim is to make it more accessible for young adults (recommended age starts from 14). The course can be completed individually due to the self-check exercises, but also applicable for blended learning mentored by educators.

GreenCool has a community on Facebook https://www.facebook.com/greencoolproject where the outputs, students' projects and tips to be green can be followed. Students also share their own green ideas on their own Instagram page.

3. The challenges

There have been a couple of challenges during the development of MOOC and the open platform. First, the common understanding of the term green and influencer had to be set. We tackled this issue through research by asking youth about who they consider an influencer and who they believe when learning about green issues. It was found that green is more than sustainability, but rather about the atmosphere and nature around us, an attitude, but at the time an overused word by companies that do greenwashing. As for influencer and influencing, youth trust the most scientists and teachers, followed by parents and peers and the least they believe what paid influencers and politicians say. The research also revealed that most youth attitudes showed the concept that humanity must adapt to the limits of nature (Kővári et al, 2023). Therefore, when developing the MOOC material, we searched for reliable scientific material as well as green influencers who are authentic and use what they preach.

The second challenge was the scale of the material. As we planned to offer the course for 1 ECTS credit we had to narrow the activities. However not to waste the information we created extra material that learners can do if they want to learn more about a topic.

The MOOC platform implementation was also a bit challenging. Although universities had experience with Moodle and University of Tartu is excellent in MOOC each platform was different and we asked local IT specialists to help with 'unpacking' and adopting the original MOOC.

The challenge at the moment is the open platform in case learners want to use it without mentors or moderators. To address this, we are creating guidelines on how to use it and also where to find help if needed.

e-Learning Excellence Awards

4. How the initiative was received

The MOOC featured two feedback questioners that helped us understand students' background and evaluate their satisfaction with the course. The first questioner was located at the very beginning of the course and collected some information on participants background (profile of their studies, how did they learn about the course and etc.). The second questioner was at the end of the course and its main goal was to access student's learning experience, overall satisfaction and areas of potential improvement.

Out of 200 students who signed up for the course, 128 have participated in the "pre-course questioner" and 41 have provided feedback in the final questioner. It is important to mention that due to usually higher drop-out rates for MOOCs, these numbers should not be surprising. Based on University of Tartu experience, only about 30-40% of initially registered participants complete the MOOC until the end. This can be due to various factors, including poor time-management skills, absence of financial penalties for not finishing the course (MOOCs at the University of Tartu are usually offered free of charge) and unpredictable factors intervening with the studies.

The MOOC was able to attract students with very diverse backgrounds. It concerns not only geographical location (as it was mentioned earlier, we had 18 countries represented in this course) (Picture 4), but also educational background. We had students from very different fields including: communication, geography, marketing, logistics, economy, IT, political science, philosophy etc. (Picture 5 and 6).

Figure 4: Participants' countries placed on the map.

Edit Kővári, Anastasiia Turusinova and Réka Vámosi

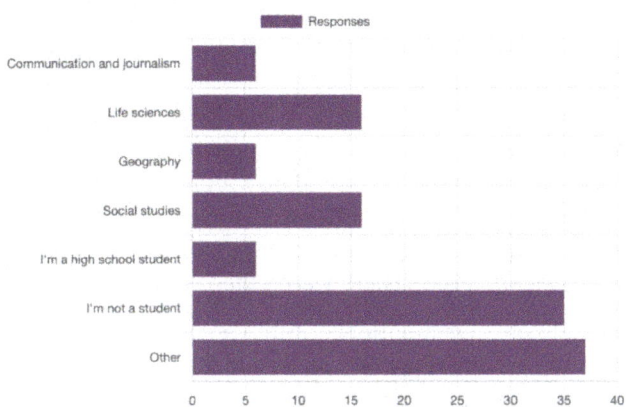

Figure 5: One of the questions in the pre-course questioner.

Figure 6: Answers to "Other" option from the previous question on the field of study.

We were also able to gather not only students, but many professionals who are already experts in the field. Many of them were working in the field of communication or sustainability and were interested in learning about the other field and how they can be connected. Unique multidisciplinary nature of the course helped to attract diverse participants and build on their expertise in a new field.

Overall, course participants provided positive feedback. 92,5% has agreed and strongly agreed that the course material on the platform was clearly organized and facilitated learning. 95,1% has agreed and strongly agreed to the statement that the course has covered the topics in an effective way. Many people mentioned that they liked the diversity of the course materials (not just text, but also many videos and visualizations) and activities (we used a wide range of different group and individual assignments). For example, it was mentioned in the feedback left by one of the students: "I really enjoyed making little videos and talking with others in forums." Another person said: "I liked that it was more than just reading the material. There were videos and different creative tasks".

One of the participants has mentioned in the anonymous feedback questioner "I really liked that there were relevant videos and a lot of extra materials that are all accessible. I liked that the modules are doable in your own pace and order". Another course participant said: "I like the different modules, which covers a wide range of topics and hence it really boosted my knowledge".

When it comes to areas of improvement, some of the participants mentioned that they would like to see even more opportunities to interact with other participants. One of the students said: "There could have been more of the tasks that encourage conversations with the other course takers". Many people also mentioned that the course was very time consuming. For example, one person said: "It took a bit more time than I would've wanted". Since the course offers nontraditional educational approaches (that don't fall under the category of just attending or watching a video lecture for 45 mins), it is expected that students are not used to it. Most of the learning was accomplished through case study analysis and interactive/creative assignments that might seem to be more time consuming. However, when designing the course, all the hours have been estimated, referring to Learning Design Toolkit by Akseli Huhtanen, Aalto University.

By the end of the course 51 students has completed all the assignments with a satisfactory grade and received a digital certificate from University of Tartu equal to 1 ECTS.

5. The learning outcomes

Educational design of the course assumed clear structure that made it easy to ensure the knowledge transfer to the course participants. Bloom's taxonomy was used to define the learning outcomes of the course and corresponding type of the exercise. Every assignment in the course was thought through to match the learning outcomes. Course authors first designed the extended course structure that includes detailed overview of the learning outcomes (Table 1) and then narrowed it down to the central learning outcomes featured in the course.

Table 1: Extended course structure.

Module	Learning Outcome	Bloom's Taxonomy	Type of Exercise
Module I: Introduction to green & communication basics	Able to **define** biodiversity & explain why it is important	knowledge	Biodiversity quiz (Lesson 1.2)
	Able to **identify** different communication models & forms	knowledge	Quiz 1.3
	Able to **distinguish** different categories of symbols	comprehension	Quiz 1.4
Module II: Craft Your Green Story	Able to **analyze** a blog based on different steps of blog creation	analysis	Quiz 2.1
	Able to **plan** a blog on a green topic	synthesis	Forum 2.1
	Able to **define** elevator pitch & its key characteristics	knowledge	Quiz 2.2
	Able to **describe** bioeconomy	knowledge	Bioeconomy quiz (Lesson 2.3)
	Able to **define** Oxford debate	knowledge	Oxford debate quiz (Lesson 2.4)
	Able to **distinguish** technical & biological cycles of circular economy	comprehension	Quiz 2.4
	Able to **analyse** TEDx talk based on different steps of its development	analysis	Quiz 2.5
Module III: Digital Video Crafting on Social Responsibility & Responsible Consumption	Able to **explain** the concept of social responsibility	comprehension	Social responsibility quiz (Lesson 3.1)
	Able to **distinguish** different video frames	comprehension	Quiz 3.2
	Able to **identify** key messages & TA of the video	comprehension	Quiz 3.2

e-Learning Excellence Awards

Module	Learning Outcome	Bloom's Taxonomy	Type of Exercise
	Able to **produce** two formats of videos	synthesis	Video submission
Module IV: Crafting your story's ethical arguments	Able to **describe** key components of sustainable living	knowledge	Sustainable living Quiz (Lesson 4.2)
	Able to **analyse** different influencers based on key persuasion principles that they use	analysis	Quiz 4.2
	Able to **identify** persuasion principles	comprehension	Forum discussion 4.2
	Able to **analyze** their own Ecological Footprint	analysis	Forum discussion 4.2
Module V: Creative communication by arts through renewable energy & smart mobility	Able to **define** renewable energy & its sources	comprehension	Quiz 5.1
	Able to **list** key events in graffiti history	knowledge	Quiz 5.2
	Able to **explain** impact of graffiti	comprehension	Forum discussion 5.2
	Able to **categorize** trash art	analysis	Art gallery post
	Able to **list** the steps of flashmob organization	knowledge	Quiz 5.4

Key learning outcomes included:

1. Able to **define** and **explain** key green environmental concepts such as circular economy, sustainability, zero waste, biodiversity, renewable energy etc.

2. Able to **define** and **explain** main communication delivery techniques such as elevator pitch, Pecha Kucha, Oxford debate and TEDx talk

3. Able to **identify** key messages and target audience of a video

4. Able to **film** and **edit** two video formats

5. Able to **analyze** different influencers based on key persuasion principles that they use

Achievement of the learning outcomes was ensured through the course activities that were carefully designed in line with them. Every course activity had a passing grade that guaranteed that students who completed the assignment – acquired the necessary knowledge and skills. To pass the course, students had to complete all the assignments and therefore achieve all the learning outcomes.

6. Plans to further develop the initiative

We have many plans in the future, as Greenfluencer for us is not just a MOOC course and GreenCool is not just a project, but a lifestyle. Therefore, we would also like to extend it outside the academic context, to other interested parties (NGOs, corporate professionals, individuals, activists, etc.), as we believe that this educational material can serve as a development tool for a large number of people. Environmental, social and governance (ESG) initiatives are getting important for companies. This means they need future employees who know the importance of the concepts, inspired to think about solution and are ready to take actions. This course can provide short and effective basic education to develop these competences. Furthermore, we aim to continue to cooperate with wider network of universities (located not just in European Capitals of Culture) to implement and further develop the ideas and the course.

References

https://greencoolproject.eu/en/home
https://www.facebook.com/greencoolproject
Kővári, E.; Formádi, K.; Banász, Z. The Green Attitude of Four European Capitals of Culture's Youth. *Sustainability* **2023**, *15*, 7866. https://doi.org/10.3390/su15107866
Huhtanen A. Learning Design Toolkit. Aalto University 2019.
https://fitech.io/app/uploads/2019/09/Learning-Design-Toolkit-v2.pdf

Author biographies

Dr Edit Kővári is a professor of human resource management at University of Pannonia, Veszprém, Hungary. She received her PhD in emotional intelligence from University of Derby, UK. Edit the National Emotional Intelligence Coordinator for Hungary at the International Society for Emotional Intelligence (ISEI). She is the secretary of the University Networks of European Capitals of Culture. She has outstanding publications, organized several international conferences. Presently her work is focusing on green attitude research and projects. Her courses and publications are mainly in communication, business ethics, emotional intelligence, cultural intelligence, FOMO and green attitude.

e-Learning Excellence Awards

Anastasiia Turusinova (MA) works as an e-learning specialist at Centre of Applied Social Sciences at Johan Skytte Institute of Political Studies, University of Tartu (Estonia). She is specializing on MOOCs (Massive Open Online Courses). She has designed more than 10 online courses for different European projects. One of her courses was nominated for the best course of the year by Estonian Quality Agency for Education (HAKA) and three of her courses received e-course quality badge from the same agency. She has been involved in evaluating online courses participating in the annual competition organized by HAKA.

Réka Vámosi (MBA) is currently working as a project manager at the Faculty of Business and Economics, University of Pannonia in Veszprém, the European Capital of Culture 2023. Her responsibilities include the full spectrum of 10+ national and international project management. She is also an accredited tour guide for the Veszprém region and proud to host the GreenLike Podcast series (www.gtk.uni-pannon.hu/hu/greenlike-podcastok).

Simulating the Complex Science Behind Environmental Hazards Like Post-wildfire Debris Flows

Keliann Laconte, Vanessa Vincente and James Russell
University Corporation for Atmospheric Research, CO, USA
klaconte@ucar.edu
vincente@ucar.edu
jamesrussell@ucar.edu

Abstract: Wildfires are an increasing danger globally and leave behind burn scars that are sensitive to flash flooding. When heavy rain falls on a burn scar, it can trigger a highly dangerous, moving mass of mud, rocks, and vegetation known as a "debris flow." The COMET Program worked with a team of subject matter experts to author two simulations and a three-dimensional (3D) animation about this environmental hazard. The simulations were authored in Articulate Storyline and published in English and Spanish on a free education and training catalog at www.meted.ucar.edu. This e-Learning initiative provides international operational forecasters with practice in using geological, hydrological, and meteorological data to evaluate conditions for a potential flash flood and debris flow event in a post-wildfire environment while raising awareness about the dangers of a lesser-known hazard. The simulation "Monitoring for Potential Flash Flood & Debris Flow Threats" includes an innovative spatial visualization approach for training. Learners use a simulated post-fire landscape, overlaid with three different types of hydrological and geological data, to connect how four key factors contribute to the likelihood of a flash flood and debris flow event occurring at a given location in that landscape. The three-dimensional visualizations allow learners to interact with data as they develop new perspectives for how the four factors interact. In the simulation "Communicating Potential Flash Flood & Debris Flow Threats," the learner takes on the role of a forecaster conversing with two different partners to understand their information needs and practice providing decision-support to each partner based on those needs. The learning outcomes are measured using pre- and post-assessments as well as user surveys. These metrics show growth as a result of the lessons and the initiative was well-received, and these results will inform the development of a third e-Learning interaction.

1. Introduction

Even after the fire is out, wildfires leave behind areas with damaged soil and vegetation called "burn scars." When rain falls within a short amount of time on a burn scar, it can trigger a highly dangerous flash flood along with a moving mass of ash, burned vegetation, and soil known as a "debris flow" (Figure 1). Wildfires occur across the U.S., and post-wildfire flash flood and debris flow events can result in loss of life and property. The significance of post-wildfire impacts motivated representatives across the U.S. National Weather Service (NWS) to form a NWS Post Wildfire Hydrology Working Group for discussing ways to improve the understanding and response to post-wildfire hazards. One of the goals of the workshop was to increase awareness on preparing for and responding to post-wildfire hazards, which served as the motivating initiative for the COMET Program in developing relevant e-Learning training resources for operational forecasters. The primary purposes of these training resources were to help forecasters better understand 1) the factors that make a post-wildfire environment conducive for flash flood and debris flow events, and 2) the critical information needs of core partners to support impact-based decision support services in response to the potential hazards.

Figure 1. In the years following a 2018 wildfire in southern Colorado, rain fell on the burned areas and flooded this county road with ash, sand, silt, trees, and boulders during a flash flood and debris flow event.

Staff in the COMET Program at the University Corporation for Atmospheric Research (UCAR) worked with a team of subject matter experts from the NWS, U.S. Geological Survey, and California Geological Survey to produce two online educational simulations and a 3D animation about this environmental hazard. Each simulation may take about an hour to complete. They are available on the MetEd website, a collection of free training resources for the geoscience community around the world.

In the simulation, "Communicating Potential Flash Flood & Debris Flow Threats," learners take on the role of a forecaster, "conversing" with two different partners to understand their information needs regarding potential debris flows events (Vincente and LaConte, 2022). Specifically, hotspot interactions were used to mimic the process of actively listening to a partner's statements to identify information that will be applied later in the simulation (see Figure 2). They then practice basic skills in providing decision-support tailored to each partner's specific needs. At this early stage of the simulation, learners receive immediate feedback from a character that acts as a coach, directing learners to job aids and providing tips on how to navigate within the learning environment. Learners reference and apply a set of four communications practices ("proactive," "audience-focused," "representative," and "clear") over the course of the lesson. The core activity of the lesson requires learners to apply those communications practices, along with specific partner needs and hydrological and meteorological data, to prepare talking points for a briefing packet tailored to each partner. To provide a more authentic challenge, learners work through multiple culminating activities before receiving delayed feedback in the form of a partner who is prepared to make decisions around potential debris flows (if the majority of responses were correct) or who is confused (if the learner was unsuccessful). The simulation provides two scenarios in which to practice and illustrate the diversity in partner roles and information needs.

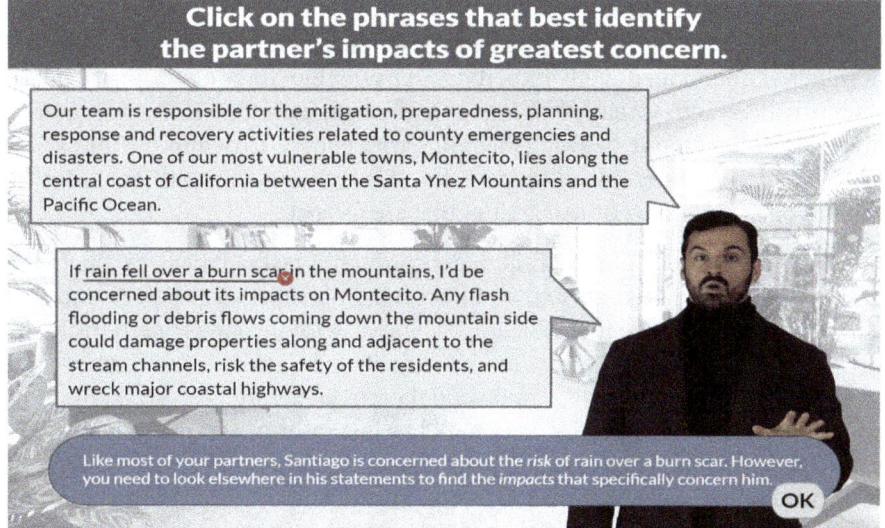

Figure 2. Screenshot from an activity in "Communicating Potential Flash Flood & Debris Flow Threats" where learners navigate a hotspot interaction, moving their cursors over statements and selecting the phrases that best express that partner's specific needs.

e-Learning Excellence Awards

In "Monitoring for Potential Flash Flood & Debris Flow Threats," learners apply intermediate skills to assess the likelihood of a debris flow occurring at different locations and times during simulated events by interacting with an innovative 3D visualization of hydrological and geological data (Vincente and LaConte, 2023). A 3D animation is provided within the monitoring simulation and separately on YouTube that summarizes the science of debris flows and the hazards they pose (University Corporation for Atmospheric Research, 2023). The animation takes viewers to the microscopic level to see how fire changes soil so that it no longer absorbs water well. Then, the viewer sees how even a small amount of rainfall can put vast amounts of material into motion. The terrain funnels water and debris — including boulders — onto a highway, with devastating impacts.

Spanish versions of the simulations, "Monitoreo del peligro potencial de inundaciones repentinas y flujos de escombros" and "Cómo comunicar el peligro potencial de crecidas repentinas y flujos de escombros," were published in 2024 (Vincente, LaConte and Russi, 2024a and 2024b).

2. The infrastructure

COMET Program staff, including an instructional designer, scientist, and graphic designer, collaborated with experts to ensure the training is instructionally, scientifically, and visually effective and engaging. COMET staff convened biweekly collaborative working meetings with experts to determine the skills that operational forecasters need to gain for this topic, along with the established science and limitations of research in this area to date.

The instructional designer led the team through a task analysis to elucidate the observable actions that an expert forecaster might perform before and after a wildfire to prevent potential catastrophic impacts to life and property from debris flows. Multiple tasks were to be conducted before wildfires occurred, underscoring the proactive and collaborative nature of decision support communications. Other tasks were to occur just prior to any precipitation events over a wildfire burn scar and involved detailed analysis of various information. In addition, the target audience is already proficient at using 2D meteorological information to construct mental models, and the task analysis process revealed that the training should focus on integrating geological and hydrological information into those existing skillsets.

This training was centered around the four components of successful learning events identified by Allen (2016): Context-Challenge-Activity-Feedback (CCAF). The CCAF model was manifested in the simulations as follows: learners were provided various cues that mimic the conditions of work as an operational forecaster (i.e., an authentic *context*). The simulations used real data from historical events, and characters were used to mimic real-life interactions with colleagues, core partners, and stakeholders. In these scenarios, learners reenacted historical events using actual burn scars and precipitation events. In some of these historical situations, debris flows occurred and led to costly impacts to property; in others, no negative impacts occurred. The online learning environment provided a safe place for learners to make mistakes as they practiced predicting whether a debris flow might occur or making preparations for such an event. The element of perceived risk gave the learner a *challenge*, and each *activity* prompted the learner to consider information and make decisions. Like in real-life, learners don't receive immediate *feedback* on whether their decisions were correct or not.

For example, the monitoring simulation applies the CCAF model to produce highly interactive analysis, synthesis, and evaluation tasks. Learners analyzed three locations on a 3D post-fire landscape that was overlaid with hydrological and geological data (Figure 3). They combined this with meteorological data during events to connect how key factors contributed to the potential for a debris flow to occur (Figure 4). The 3D visualizations allowed learners to interact with data as they developed new perspectives for how key geological, hydrological, and meteorological factors interact. Next, they were prompted to answer questions such as "Are you concerned about the soil burn severity across the landscape for this location?" and "Does the hourly rainfall accumulation suggest that the rainfall rate threshold has been or will be met or exceeded at this location?" Learners must answer multiple questions correctly before a character provides positive feedback about how the learner has successfully integrated two of the key factors (Figure 5).

e-Learning Excellence Awards

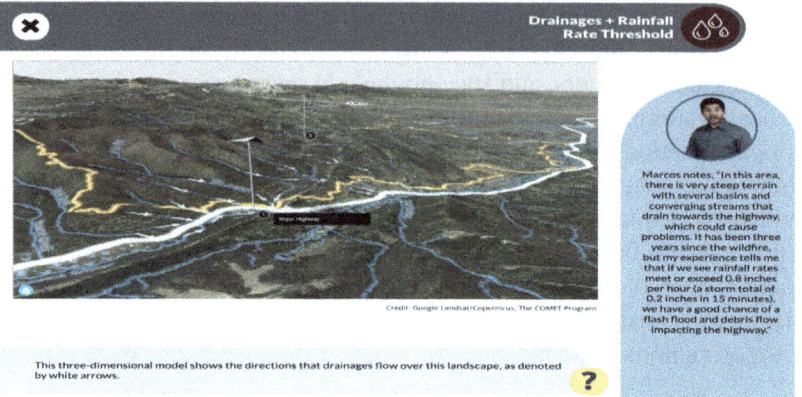

Figure 3. An example view from an interactive tool in "Monitoring for Potential Flash Flood & Debris Flow Threats" where learners enlarge, rotate, zoom, and pan around a 3D model to better understand the characteristics of an area impacted by the wildfire. White arrows denote the directions that drainages flow over this landscape. A character on the right side of the interactive represents a collaborator that provides details on rainfall rate thresholds for flash flood and debris flow events.

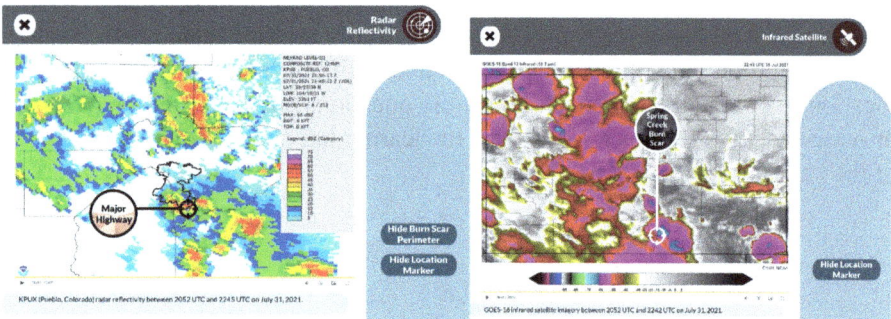

Figure 4. An example of two meteorological datasets that learners analyze in "Monitoring for Potential Flash Flood & Debris Flow Threats." Both radar reflectivity (left) and infrared satellite imagery (right) provide information about developing convection that may exceed rainfall rate thresholds for flash flood and debris flow potential.

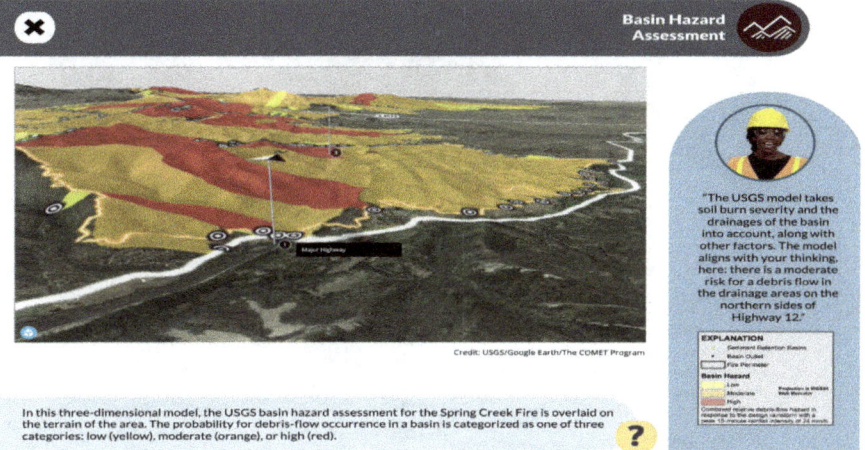

Figure 5. Screenshot from an activity in "Monitoring for Potential Flash Flood & Debris Flow Threats" where learners use the 3D model to assess the risk of a debris flow in the drainage area of interest. A character on the right side of the interactive represents a collaborator that provides positive feedback about successfully using this type of data.

The team used an iterative design process where initial drafts of activities were displayed on Google Slides or Articulate Review servers for multiple rounds of review. Experts provided specific recommendations for improvements on every screen of the simulation. For the 3D animation, a graphic designer used Autodesk 3D Studio Max, Nextlimit Realflow 10, and FumeFX 5 to model a canyon using drone footage and add fluid and debris flowing down it. Experts provided input on the characteristics of the flow and type of debris to ensure that it accurately represented the process and the ultimate impacts on a nearby highway (Figure 6). The final simulations were exported as HTML5 packages and published to the MetEd website.

Figure 6. Screenshot of a 3D animation that models how rain triggered a debris flow event in Glenwood Canyon, Colorado in 2021. Through collaboration with experts, the training team created scientifically accurate text and visuals to explain the complex processes behind debris flows.

3. The challenges

A variety of roles and tasks are involved in post-wildfire situations, and it was necessary to convene multiple discussions with experts on this topic during the initial stages of simulation development. In particular, the training team was informed about the responsibilities of operational forecasters in monitoring meteorological conditions and assessing debris flow potentials, service hydrologists in tailoring warnings thresholds and identifying high risk areas, and officials who evaluate burned landscapes and assets at risk to wildfire impacts. Understanding the areas of expertise, how information was collected, and how event details were communicated to core partners was critical to the scientific composition and instructional design of the training products and ensure an effective learning experience.

Additionally, much effort was dedicated to designing visualizations that represented the conceptual understanding of debris flow initiation and the layers of information involved in assessing the potential for a debris flow event. Training staff explored data resources to gather soil burn severity, burn scar perimeter, and basin hazard data in formats suitable for visualization in Google Earth and Sketchfab. The training staff worked closely with the experts to ensure the scientific accuracy and digestibility of the conceptual animations and 3D model frameworks that forecasters mentally develop for situational awareness and forecasting operations.

The team had multiple discussions about how to account for the many unknowns regarding the science of debris flows and the underlying complexities of geology, hydrology, and meteorology. The team ultimately decided to focus the simulation on the state of the science at the time and encourage forecasters to always issue a warning if there is a chance that one of these catastrophic events could occur.

4. How the initiative was received

The simulations and 3D animation were well-received by learners, as recorded by traffic to the site as the number of individual "sessions" — an instance where the simulation was used for more than one minute and at least two pages were accessed — as well as through learner surveys.

The English versions of the simulations have received ongoing traffic in the months since they were published. The communication simulation was viewed in 423 sessions over the course of 20 months; over the course of 15 months, the monitoring simulation was also viewed in 423 sessions. However, traffic to the Spanish simulations was low, in part due to their more recent publication date. The Spanish communications simulation was viewed in 14 sessions and the monitoring simulation in 50 (University Corporation for Atmospheric Research, 2024). Table 1 shows the total number of sessions for each simulation on MetEd, along with the total numbers of post-tests completed and the number of months between publication and the time of data analysis.

Table 1. For each simulation, the total number of sessions on MetEd is provided, along with the total numbers of post-tests completed and the number of months between publication and the time of data analysis.

Simulation	Total MetEd sessions	Total post-test completions on MetEd	Number of months that data was collected
Communicating Potential Flash Flood & Debris Flow Threats	423	242	20
Monitoring for Potential Flash Flood & Debris Flow Threats	423	221	15

e-Learning Excellence Awards

Simulation	Total MetEd sessions	Total post-test completions on MetEd	Number of months that data was collected
Cómo comunicar el peligro potencial de crecidas repentinas y flujos de escombros	14	12	6
Monitoreo del peligro potencial de inundaciones repentinas y flujos de escombros	50	26	6

A small sample of learner surveys are available for the English versions of the simulations and indicate that learners perceive the simulations to be effective and interesting. 89% of 82 respondents on the communications simulation and 83% of 75 respondents on the monitoring simulation agreed or strongly agreed that the format was effective for learning. Notably, learners agreed to strongly agreed that "[t]he lesson contained particularly interesting, useful and/or well-designed elements" (92% of respondents for the communication simulation and 87% of respondents for the monitoring simulation) (University Corporation for Atmospheric Research, 2024).

The 3D animation, hosted on YouTube, is the top-viewed asset on the COMET Program channel, with 2,400 views in one year (University Corporation for Atmospheric Research, 2023). The popularity of this resource suggests that it is at a minimum raising awareness about a lesser known but increasingly common hazard.

5. The learning outcomes

The results of the task analysis were used to specify learning objectives (below) and create realistic feedback within the simulation to show the learner specifically where they performed correctly and where they needed improvement. The simulation was structured so that the learner could not proceed without correcting their most significant mistakes, ensuring that learners who completed it had achieved some level of proficiency with the content.

Communicating Potential Flash Flood & Debris Flow Threats

- *Identify the primary partner information needs for post-fire debris flow events*

- Use hydrological and meteorological data to convey potential post-fire threats and impacts to a partner
- Implement promising practices for decision support communications during post-fire debris flow events

Monitoring for Potential Flash Flood & Debris Flow Threats

- Weigh the four factors that are key to monitor for potential debris flows in post-wildfire burn areas:
    - Soil burn severity across the landscape
    - Drainages across the landscape
    - Potential for heavy rainfall
    - Potential to meet or exceed the rainfall rate threshold
- Use geological, hydrological and meteorological data to evaluate conditions for a potential debris flow event in a post-wildfire environment
- Identify the contributions made by of the Burned Area Emergency Response (BAER) Team, hydrologists and forecasters in assessing the potential for debris flow events in a post-wildfire burn area

Pre- and post-test data were collected for each of the four simulations to evaluate the learning outcomes. Each pre-test consisted of a subset of questions from the simulation and the post-test consisted of entirely new questions. Like the simulation itself, the tests were scenario-based. Initial test questions were drafted to align with the cognitive tasks that learners were expected to perform, the lesson objectives, and the lesson content. Science and instruction experts reviewed the questions and provided suggestions. The revised tests were published with the simulation and learners were prompted to complete them as they navigated to and from the simulation, but the tests were optional and not required for completing the simulation. An item analysis was conducted on the post-test questions several months later to help test for reliability, and Point-Biserial Correlation Coefficient scores indicate that learners who pass are not attracted to the wrong answers (University Corporation for Atmospheric Research, 2024).

Table 2 shows the number of learners who took both the pre- and post-test for any of the debris flow simulations on MetEd and their mean pre- and post-test scores and standard deviations (SD). While over half of learners completed post-tests for communications and monitoring simulations, only a subset of this total completed *both* a pre- and post-test (85 and 77, respectively). For this subset of data, the affiliations reported by each of these learners was coded as either a professional category (e.g., International Meteorological or Hydrologic Service, College/University Faculty) or non-professional (e.g., College/University Student, Weather Enthusiast). The data is reported separately for each of these two affiliation categories.

Table 2. The number of learners who completed both the pre- and post-tests is reported along with their mean scores and standard deviations (SD). The score gain was calculated and reported as a percentage. The data for those who were categorized under either a professional or non-professional affiliation are each also reported separately.

Communicating Potential Flash Flood & Debris Flow Threats

	Mean pre-test score *(SD)*	Mean post-test score *(SD)*	Score gain (%)
Total (n=85)	76 *(19)*	83 *(12)*	7%
Professionals (n=31, or 36% of the total)	81 *(17)*	85 *(12)*	3%
Non-professionals (n=53, or 64% of the total)	73 *(19)*	83 *(12)*	10%

Monitoring for Potential Flash Flood & Debris Flow Threats

	Mean pre-test score *(SD)*	Mean post-test score *(SD)*	Score gain (%)
Total (n=77)	76 *(17)*	86 *(12)*	10%
Professionals (n=30, or 39% of the total)	83 *(15)*	91 *(7)*	8%
Non-professionals (n=47, or 61% of the total)	72 *(17)*	83 *(13)*	11%

The results show positive gains for learners (also reported in Table 2). The MetEd user community consists of a large percentage of university students, weather enthusiasts, and other non-professional categories, and these learners especially benefited from the simulations. For the communications simulation, the group's improvement of post-test over pre-test was 7%, with professionals gaining only

3% and non-professionals, 10%. For the monitoring simulation, the improvement was 10%. These gains were clear for both professional and non-professional groups, increasing 8% and 11%, respectively. The majority of learners were affiliated with a non-professional category (64% for the communications simulation and 61% for the monitoring simulation, respectively), indicating that the topic has broad appeal beyond the professional audiences it was designed to reach. Professionals also benefit from the simulations, with the monitoring simulation having the highest gains (8%) and lowest variation from the mean (SD=7). For this category, the communication simulation saw gains of only 3%, potentially due to the fact that the content is at a basic level, whereas the monitoring simulation targets intermediate skills.

It is not possible to make generalizations on the outcomes of the Spanish-language versions of the simulations; the simulations were published in 2024 and the sample size is small: only 3 and 8 learners completed both the pre- and post-tests for the communications and monitoring simulations, respectively (University Corporation for Atmospheric Research, 2024). However, as more learners complete the pre- and post-tests for all of the simulations, the data will be used to inform future simulations.

6. Plans to further develop the initiative

A team of instructional designers, scientists, a graphic designer, and subject matter experts developed two simulations and a 3D animation on debris flows, a lesser known but increasingly dangerous environmental hazard. These resources effectively increased practical communications and forecasting skills for these events. The previous two simulations immersed the learner in the process of communicating with partners before a debris flow event and then predicting a flash flood and debris flow event as it happened. Learners proceeded through a sequence of analyses and judgements. They saw the consequences of their actions — whether right or wrong — and then received guidance on how to be more effective in the future. Evaluation results show the effectiveness of these innovative teaching methods to improve learning. The COMET Program will work with experts to develop a third e-Learning component that will focus on working with an interdisciplinary team to assess post-wildfire areas for debris flows. This component, like the previous two, will be simulation-based, providing the learner an immersive experience in learning about debris flows.

References

Allen, M. W. (2016) Michael Allen's Guide to E-Learning : Building Interactive, Fun, and Effective Learning Programs for Any Company. Second edition. Hoboken, New Jersey: John Wiley & Sons.

University Corporation for Atmospheric Research/The COMET Program (2023) Recipe for disaster: Flash flooding mobilizes dangerous debris flows on fire-scarred slopes. Available at https://youtu.be/aHLhGKT5vmY?si=Gsa_b0j9HF-E-RIU (Accessed July 1, 2024).

University Corporation for Atmospheric Research/The COMET Program. (2024). MetEd Reports. Unpublished aggregate internal company data.

Vincente, V. and LaConte, K. (2022) Communicating Potential Flash Flood & Debris Flow Threats. Available at: https://www.meted.ucar.edu/education_training/lesson/10163 (Accessed July 1, 2024).

Vincente, V. and LaConte, K. (2023) Monitoring for Potential Flash Flood & Debris Flow Threats. Available at: https://www.meted.ucar.edu/education_training/lessons/10162 (Accessed July 1, 2024).

Vincente, V., LaConte, K. and Russi, D. (2024a) Cómo comunicar el peligro potencial de crecidas repentinas y flujos de escombros. Available at: https://www.meted.ucar.edu/education_training/lessons/10258 (Accessed July 1, 2024).

Vincente, V., LaConte, K. and Russi, D. (2024b) Monitoreo del peligro potencial de inundaciones repentinas y flujos de escombros. Available at: https://www.meted.ucar.edu/education_training/lessons/10255 (Accessed July 1, 2024).

Author biographies

Keliann LaConte has spent the last 15 years leading education and research projects that provide training to deepen critical thinking and creativity in science and engineering fields. She is currently a senior educational designer with The COMET Program working to create online learning environments that make training more impactful.

Vanessa Vincente is an Associate Scientist for The COMET Program, where she works with a talented team of instructional designers, graphic artists, and multimedia developers to create customized and practical training resources for diverse audiences working in geoscience disciplines such as hydrology, tropical weather, and satellite meteorology.

Keliann LaConte, Vanessa Vincente and James Russell

James Russell is an Associate Scientist for The COMET Program. He is a meteorologist with expertise in a variety of weather and climate topics. He manages hydrology projects for COMET and works with a talented team to produce training resources in meteorology, oceanography, and hydrology.

XP Boost: Empowering Generation Alpha's Food Literacy

Nadine du Piesanie, Nadene Marx-Pienaar, Nadine Sonnenberg and Adeline Pretorius
Department of Consumer and Food Sciences, University of Pretoria, South Africa
nadinedp96@gmail.com
nadene.marxp@up.ac.za
nadine.sonnenberg@up.ac.za
adeline.pretorius@up.ac.za

Abstract: Globally, Generation Alpha (born since 2010) is growing up in convenience-centric food environments, placing them at risk for the triple burden of malnutrition. Food illiteracy exacerbates this issue. On the flip side, food literacy is the competency needed to make healthy choices; hence, lack thereof might highlight the need for intervention if healthier futures are the ultimate goal. Traditional educational methods often fail to engage this tech-savvy demographic on topics such as food and dietary practices, necessitating the exploration of alternative solutions such as gamification. Gamification integrates game mechanics into non-game contexts, such as e-learning platforms, to capture Generation Alpha's attention in an enjoyable and meaningful way, thereby boosting engagement in food literacy initiatives. This case study presents an initiative that developed an RPG (role-playing game) using RPG Maker MV software, specifically designed to assess and improve food literacy among Generation Alpha participants. Preliminary results indicate the game's successful engagement with users and ability to serve as an effective food literacy assessment tool. Future plans include integrating eye-tracking technology to enhance engagement further and support children with learning disabilities.

1. Introduction

Generation Alpha is reaching adulthood in a rapidly advancing, technology-driven world dominated by overconsumption of fast food and digital distractions, sidelining essential life skills such as cooking and sustainable food choices (Carruba et al., 2022). This deficiency in basic skills and knowledge when it comes to food and nutrition manifests in alarming ways, with a noticeable increase in higher-than-optimal BMI levels and a concerning surge in deaths attributed to noncommunicable diseases (NCDs) such as cardiovascular diseases, diabetes, and cancers (Parekh et al., 2020). These issues are further exacerbated by factors such as busy family schedules, declining intergenerational culinary knowledge transfer, limited comprehensive food education in schools and the pervasive influence of convenience food services like Uber Eats (Okumus, 2021).

e-Learning Excellence Awards

This convergence has created a significant disconnect between nutrition and food preparation principles and underscores the pressing need for innovative educational approaches to bridge this gap. Food illiteracy is not merely a lack of cooking skills; it encompasses a broader inability to make informed food choices, understand nutritional information, and appreciate the environmental impact of our dietary habits (Silva, 2023). Food literacy is the ability to navigate a complex food environment and involves using food and nutrition knowledge, skills, and behaviours to achieve optimal dietary quality and health (Poelman et al., 2018). It encompasses four key domains: planning and managing, selecting, preparing, and eating food. This gap in knowledge poses significant risks not only to general health and well-being but also impacts ecological sustainability, economic stability, cultural preservation, social equity, food security, ethical consumption, and a sense of global responsibility. The problem is further complicated by the fact that conventional educational styles are currently implemented to rectify the issue but often lack the ability to successfully engage this younger generation (Maulida and Malik, 2022).

Many educational institutions still employ traditional learning, teaching, and evaluation approaches that may induce disinterest and stress in students (Fernando and Premadasa, 2024). Saqib and Rehman (2023) conceptualise academic stress as a multifaceted construct that includes educational anxiety, pressure, and stress associated with the preparation for assessments such as exams, tests, homework, reading, and an overload of academic work. Elevated levels of academic stress have been shown to impair cognitive function, attention, and memory retrieval, thereby hindering students' ability to concentrate, process information, and retain new knowledge (Saqib et al., 2023). In the context of food literacy, this impairment can significantly affect students' capacity to assimilate critical information related to nutrition, sustainable food practices, and informed dietary choices. Ideally, children's academic journeys should be an enriching experience that fosters life skills (Drugas, 2022). Unfortunately, the current educational style/ environment is not conducive to this; hence, it is experienced as a challenge that negatively impacts Generation Alpha's development. Therefore, an urgent call for innovative approaches that could engage students in food literacy in schools and other educational platforms is much needed. This includes developing comprehensive educational strategies tailored to the unique needs and interests of Generation Alpha and integrating interactive and practical learning experiences to promote a deeper understanding of food and nutrition. Mark Rober's TED talk delved into the 'Super Mario Effect,' urging individuals to embrace challenges and actively pursue knowledge enthusiastically rather than shy away from learning obstacles (Rober, 2018).

Globally, games have taken off under Generation Alpha, with Newzoo gaming insights reporting that 9 out of 10, Gen Alpha and Gen Z are game enthusiasts. In South Africa, 38% of Generation Alpha regularly engage in online gaming, supporting the fact that this growing interest in gaming should be viewed as an opportunity to engage this specific cohort (Jakob, 2024). By integrating elements of games into education, gamification sparks motivation and participation, turning learning into an interactive adventure. Integration of game mechanics into non-game contexts, such as e-learning platforms and learning management systems, offers much potential to captivate Generation Alpha's attention in a meaningful and enjoyable manner, thus enhancing their participation in initiatives devoted to assessing and improving food literacy (Katsagoni et al., 2019).

2. The infrastructure

To successfully engage and motivate Generation Alpha, this initiative used RPG Maker MV software to develop and create an RPG (roleplay game), fully deployable on all Windows, Mac, and mobile devices. RPG Maker software is a free-to-use, open-source game development engine incorporating Java Script in combination with HTML5 export (Maker, 2023). It was primarily chosen for its ease of use, versatility and broader platform compatibility. The game title "Sprouts: Quest Towards a Healthier Future" is an interactive fiction game inspired by narrative exposition-based games with an adventure-based storyline. The game requires choices to be made in order to move the game forward. To limit the design effort, the choices are considered snap decisions that do not alter the storytelling but are still relevant to the flow. According to research, good storytelling evokes powerful emotions that aid in connecting with the characters, allowing for a deeper, more immersive, and more impactful experience (Wolfe et al., 2022).

According to cyberpsychology, immersion within video games is a common occurrence and is the trademark of a well-executed plot. Studies confirmed this as players reported that they felt most absorbed playing games with strategic components that contribute to narrative elements, as they want to solve the problem in order to find out more about the storyline and explore a new environment (Naul and Liu, 2020).

Sprout's storyline follows the adventures of Billy, where players are presented with choices related to food as a part of the narrative in order to move the story forward and explore new, exciting environments. This story first takes place in a small village where Billy discovers that his mother has to work a double shift, placing the responsibility of caring for his siblings on his shoulders. The first challenge of the game and set of choices is related to the plan and manage aspect of food literacy. Billy asks the player for help finding a recipe in his vast library of books and then plans what breakfast to prepare. The player is presented with a set of healthy and unhealthy choices, for example, the choice between ordering something from Uber Eats, making waffles and ice cream or making a balanced breakfast of eggs, toast and fruit. Through the progression of the game various levels/ environments are unlocked for the player to explore and engage with. These environments are riddles with Easter eggs (a secret feature placed inside a game that is usually hidden from the public eye until it is discovered by the players, often as a strange occurrence or extra collectables) that are not necessarily essential to the game story but add an extra layer of excitement and enjoyability to the game (Takbiri et al., 2023).

3. Features within the game included:

Avatar: Sprouts kicks off with an 'introduction' cut scene where the player gets to customise and personalise their own in-game avatar completely. This feature allows players to give their avatar a nickname, select its gender, and change its body shape, hairstyle and colour, facial features, and clothes. Inspired by 'The Sims' game, which incorporated these extensive customisation features to increase enjoyment, autonomy, control and player attachment. Furthermore, avatar customisation was also found to help players engage with the content more eagerly and led to improved learning outcomes (Cuthbert et al., 2019).

Figure 1: Avatar customisation

Free Exploration: Sprouts allows players to navigate around the game map freely with a simple click on the screen or area (alternatively using the Arrow keys or W, A, S, and D keys on the keyboard). The NPC (non-player characters) are scattered around the map to offer guidance and tips on progressing through the game should the player get stuck. Once the main objective has been achieved within each exploration area, the player will automatically be allowed to progress to the next objective and environment on the map.

Figure 2: Small town for player to explore

Game music and sound effects: Time perception, or rather, biassed time perception, has been framed as a valuable indication of immersion and engagement in games. Music generally has a strong yet subjective effect on our emotions; for example, it can reduce anxiety, focus attention, and allow players to have an overall sensory immersion into the game (Nuyens et al., 2020). 'Sprouts' aimed to facilitate immersion and enjoyment, induce emotions, and affect player behaviour by including royalty-free background music, which changes with every new environment entered, and sound effects where appropriate, for example, the sound of footsteps or doors opening and closing.

Feedback mechanisms: Various mechanisms provide positive feedback about the player's progress via the in-game event book and minimap on the top right side of the screen. Extra features and Easter eggs are scattered within each map/environment for the player to find and explore. These extra mechanics and features include various battles (which progress the player XP) and coins (to buy more snacks at the tuckshops and grocery store), mirrors to allow for avatar dress up or clothes change and entertaining NPC interactions. These extra features and discoveries will have no purpose but to strengthen positive rewards and interaction. In the game's last objective area (Billy's dining room), upon successfully completing the main storyline, a celebratory ceremony with fireworks will be held, and players will be congratulated and given their final food literacy score. This final cutscene of the score will also invoke a sense of competitiveness to improve or outdo their friends in the next play.

4. The challenges

While the goal of this initiative seemed fairly straightforward, it was not without challenges. Firstly, in the design and development of the game, it was realised that gamification is not a one-size-fits-all solution. It required a careful blend of educational and assessment objectives and game design customised for the specific target player, in this case, generation alpha. The primary aim of this initiative was to promote interaction, engagement and enjoyment, revolutionising conventional assessments and instruction into dynamic experiences. The initiative focused on crafting a game that aligned with current trends and emulated the allure of generation alphas' beloved games with popular titles such as Super Mario, Minecraft, Fallout, or Skyrim. In contrast to traditional educational games like Kahoot!, these games are meticulously tailored to captivate generation alpha players. The main challenge to overcome was to create a game that would allow players:

1. The freedom to fail
2. The freedom to experiment, explore and discover new strategies and pieces of information
3. The freedom to assume different identities and encourage players to see problems from a different perspective
4. The freedom of effort: to invoke a sense of critical thinking as players reflect on tasks they have accomplished.

Once the game was developed, several glitches emerged before a "playable" version of the game was launched. Resolving these glitches required extensive playtesting. Testing in the context of video games means conducting internal testing in order to test the game's usability and playability, whereby testing methods are specific to each prototype stage (Ramadan and Widyani, 2013). Sprouts made use of formal detail playtesting, whereby the feature functionality and game difficulty were tested. (operations testing) Playtesters who initially played early versions of the game identified several bugs, dead ends, loopholes and glitches within the game that caused errors and, in some cases, prevented the player from progressing to the next level. Furthermore playtesters commented on the difficulty level of the various stages of the game as well as the dialogue. These challenges were documented and addressed by refining the game code and making dialogue simpler and more enjoyable to read and follow. Once addressed,

Closed Beta testing commenced, which is the playtesting of the prototype game to help identify and fix critical problems relating to gamer interface and engagement. During beta testing, feedback was gathered related to fun, overall engagement, and suitability towards Generation Alpha. It was discovered that the game time was too long due to additional fun features, such as extensive choices for player avatar customisation. Furthermore, it was discovered that the younger generation of alphas struggled to read and follow along with the narrative, extending game time. In essence, extended game time is not necessarily a concern; however, when collecting data or using it as an assessment tool, this needs to be addressed to avoid compromising data reliability. To combat this, the initial idea was to create two versions of the game 1. That educates, and 2. The assessment. However, by shortening the storyline and removing avatar customisation and easter eggs, game completion could be achieved in a much shorter timespan.

Another challenge presented itself in measuring food literacy in the game. This required the integration of a structured questionnaire that measured the player's knowledge, skills and behaviour in terms of each of the four dimensions of food literacy, including planning, selecting, preparing and eating (Poelman et al., 2018; Amin et al., 2018). Care was taken to include sufficient scale items about each dimension of food literacy. In total, the instrument included 72 scale items. Scale items were embedded as in-game questions, prompting the player to respond by selecting one of 5 answers in line with the original measuring instrument's 5-point Likert-type agreement scale. Structuring the measuring instrument in this manner allowed for a final calculation of each player's overall food literacy score. More importantly, it also allowed for scoring each of the four dimensions separately, highlighting potential areas of concern. In following the guidelines proposed by Khorramrouz et al. (2022, final food literacy scores were categorised as low (≤ 58), medium (>58), and high (≥ 81). To ensure the food literacy measurement tool was well-integrated into the game and favourably received by the players, each food literacy question was combined with quirky banter and some generation-specific slang to make the questions fun and more relatable.

5. Pilot testing and participant feedback

Before play testing commenced, a cognitive focus group was conducted with 14 Generation alphas (aged 12-14) to validate the traditional food literacy questionnaire questions. Participants provided feedback on formatting, layout, length, and question clarity, ensuring that questions were not offensive or threatening. This feedback was subsequently integrated into the in-game questionnaire. Following this, the game underwent qualitative piloting with 30 Generation Alpha participants, aged 9 to 13, after completing playtesting. Revisions were made to address concerns related to game duration and technical issues identified during playtesting. The pilot results demonstrated high levels of user engagement and enjoyment, as reflected in both verbal feedback from the participants, who expressed enthusiasm for sharing and comparing scores, and observational data, which indicated strong nonverbal indicators of immersion and sustained interest. Several participants even requested the addition of an expansion pack. Overall, the pilot revealed that the story-embedded questions within the game facilitated an engaging and novel learning experience, encouraging active participation, critical thinking, and the extension of the participants' existing knowledge.

6. The learning outcomes

In gamification research, learning outcomes are most often measured by motivation, engagement, and academic performance. Academic performance reflects the improvement of students' ability to acquire and apply knowledge, while motivation is crucial for shaping focus and effort in learning activities (Li et al., 2023). Engagement signifies the amount of time, commitment, and involvement students spend on a task, which contributes to the overall success of learning outcomes. "Sprouts" has achieved learning outcomes in two ways: 1) A platform for educators to use in assessment, 2) engagement and education about food literacy and applications thereof.

For educators, game-based assessments could replace conventional methods that grapple with hard-to-measure, complex skills such as creative thinking and problem-solving. Where current traditional assessments failed to evaluate multifaceted constructs such as food literacy, this game shows great promise. Because of the interactive nature, it allowed for a more holistic evaluation of their abilities (Fernando and Premadasa, 2024). Furthermore, it provided insights into their problem-solving strategies, adaptability, and creativity within the context of food literacy. Apart from assessing these skills, they can also be further developed and refined through realistic in-game scenarios. This not only boosts students' knowledge but also motivates them to apply what they've learned in practical ways. For instance, after playing the game, students may show an interest in creating a shopping list or budget, making better selections of seasonal fruits and vegetables at the store, and more effectively comprehending and interpreting food labels.

Questions embedded in stories provided students with a fresh and exciting learning and assessment experience, guiding them to participate actively and think critically and aiding them in using their knowledge better. In addition, each food literacy question was combined with quirky banter and some generation-specific slang to make the questions fun and more relatable. For instance, within the game, players might face a scenario where they choose to purchase only sweets at the in-game tuckshop. As a consequence of this decision, their character would experience diminished stamina and energy levels during subsequent boss battles, causing sluggish movements and slower reaction times due to a blood sugar crash. This physical downturn within the game would be an immediate, tangible consequence of their food choice. In response, a non-player character (NPC) would intervene, offering corrective feedback and advising the player to select healthier options in the future. The NPC might explain that fruits and vegetables would provide more sustained energy, thereby improving the player's endurance and performance in the game. For example, the NPC would share fun facts about the benefits of bananas as a quick energy booster or how leafy greens improve overall vitality, linking these benefits directly to improved gameplay outcomes such as increased stamina and quicker recovery. This combination of dynamic feedback and educational reinforcement corrects poor decisions and fosters a deeper understanding of food literacy. By embedding learning within the gameplay, the initiative helps players internalise the connection between food choices and performance, promoting knowledge retention and positive behavioural change. This hands-on experience in the game translates to tangible and practical skills that students can use in their day-to-day lives.

The measurement of food literacy relied on a structured questionnaire to assess players' knowledge, skills, and behaviour in four key dimensions: planning, selecting, preparing, and eating. The design of the food literacy scale drew from previous studies and measuring instruments to ensure its validity and reliability. The questionnaire incorporated scale items and anchoring from the Food and Nutrition Literacy (FNLIT) and Expanded Food and Nutrition Education Program (EFNEP) behaviour checklist (Doustmohammadian et al., 2017, Bradford et al., 2010). A cognitive focus group was conducted with 14 generation alphas aged 12-14 to validate the food literacy questionnaire questions. Participants provided feedback on formatting, layout, length, and question clarity, ensuring that questions were not offensive or threatening. Feedback from the focus group was then integrated into the in-game questionnaire.

Care was taken to include sufficient scale items pertaining to each dimension of food literacy. In total, the instrument included 72 scale items. Scale items were embedded as in-game questions, prompting the player to respond by selecting one of 5 answers. This was because the original measuring instrument included a 5-point Likert-type agreement scale. Structuring the measuring instrument in this manner allowed for a final calculation of an overall food literacy score for each respondent/player. More importantly, it also allowed for scoring each of the four dimensions separately, highlighting potential areas of concern.

To interpret the food literacy of the players/group, this initiative relied on the proposal made by Khorramrouz (2021), who determined the optimal food literacy cut-off score using a receiver operating characteristic (ROC) analysis. Final food literacy scores were categorised as low (≤ 58), medium (>58), and high (≥ 81) (Khorramrouz et al., 2022).

Reflecting on the specific objective set for this initiative, the results were twofold. First and foremost, it revealed areas of concern pertaining to Generation Alpha's food literacy, i.e. selection is a dimension where intervention is much needed, and future initiatives can expand on this. Secondly, results underscored that gamification as an education tool is definitely more successful compared to conventional/traditional methods when multidimensional constructs such as food literacy need to be taught or measured. This style of teaching seemed to instil a sense of autonomy amongst this group of players, which allowed them to explore without fear of failure. This has been proven to foster greater retention of information, and hence, we believe ensures long-term success.

7. Future Plans

Future plans involve adapting the game to incorporate virtual reality (VR), with the aim of enhancing participant immersion. This adaptation is expected to create a more realistic experience by enabling physical interaction and movement, thereby potentially increasing the tool's effectiveness and success in creating healthier lifestyles.

In terms of measurement potential, eye-tracking technology is thought to be included. This will provide a deeper insight into underlying responses that are not necessarily measured or revealed by traditional research methods. When combining VR and eye-tracking, the combination can be particularly advantageous when considering individuals with disabilities. This innovation follows the player's eyes, eliminating the need for hand use, which opens up new opportunities for students with learning disabilities, such as ADHD and Dyslexia, offering them an equitable chance to learn and be assessed (Chan et al., 2022).

To conclude, it is believed that by leveraging the principles of educational game design, combined with the capabilities of digital tools and platforms, researchers are on the verge of developing a cost-effective, time-efficient strategy to enhance student engagement and reduce the anxiety associated with conventional assessments. The potential of gamification to significantly improve learning outcomes and increase student motivation is substantial.

References

Amin, S. A. P. M. P. H., Panzarella, C. M. S. M. P. H., Lehnerd, M. M. S., Cash, S. B. P., Economos, C. D. P. & Sacheck, J. M. P. 2018. Identifying Food Literacy Educational Opportunities for Youth. *Health Education & Behavior, 45,* 918-925.

Carruba, A. G. M., Azevedo, A. C. P. D. & Barreto, M. A. M. 2022. Learning in the 21st century: The development of critical thinking of the alpha generation. *International Journal of Human Sciences Research, 2,* 2-12.

Chan, A. S., Lee, T.-L., Sze, S. L., Yang, N. S. & Han, Y. M. 2022. Eye-tracking training improves the learning and memory of children with learning difficulty. *Scientific Reports, 12,* 13974.

Cuthbert, R., Turkay, S. & Brown, R. The effects of customisation on player experiences and motivation in a virtual reality game. Proceedings of the 31st Australian Conference on Human-Computer-Interaction, 2019. 221-232.

Drugas, M. 2022. Screenagers or" Screamagers"? Current Perspectives on Generation Alpha. *Psychological Thought, 15,* 1.

Fernando, P. A. & Premadasa, H. S. 2024a. Use of gamification and game-based learning in educating Generation Alpha. *Educational Technology & Society, 27,* 114-132.

Fernando, P. A. & Premadasa, H. S. 2024b. Use of gamification and game-based learning in educating Generation Alpha: A systematic literature review. *Educational Technology & Society, 27,* 114-132.

Jakob, J. 2024. Gen Alpha & Gen Z: The Future of Gaming *Newzoo gamer insights* Newzoo.

Katsagoni, C. N., Apostolou, A., Georgoulis, M., Psarra, G., Bathrellou, E., Filippou, C., Panagiotakos, D. B., Sidossis, L. S. D. O. K., Health, D. O. L. S. S. O. A. & Sciences, R. U. T. S. U. O. N. J. N. B. N. J. 2019. Schoolteachers' Nutrition Knowledge, Beliefs, and Attitudes Before and After an E-Learning Program. *Journal of Nutrition Education and Behavior, 51,* 1088-1098.

Khorramrouz, F., Doustmohammadian, A., Amini, M., Sarivi, S. P., Khadem-Rezaiyan, M., Moghadam, M. R. S. F. & Khosravi, M. 2022. Validity of a modified food and nutrition literacy questionnaire in primary school children in Iran. *British Journal of Nutrition, 127,* 1588-1597.

Maker, R. 2023. RPG Maker MV. WindowsR 7/8/8.1/10 (32bit/64bit) ed. Steam

Li, M., Ma, S. & Shi, Y. 2023. Examining the effectiveness of gamification as a tool promoting teaching and learning in educational settings: a meta-analysis. *Frontiers in Psychology, 14,* 1253549.

Maulida, A. Z. & Malik, M. S. 2022. Nutrition education in alpha generation to achieve optimal growth and development. *Cakrawala Dini: Jurnal Pendidikan Anak Usia Dini, 12,* 185-194.

e-Learning Excellence Awards

Naul, E. & Liu, M. 2020. Why story matters: A review of narrative in serious games. *Journal of Educational Computing Research,* 58**,** 687-707.

Nuyens, F. M., Kuss, D. J., Lopez-Fernandez, O. & Griffiths, M. D. 2020. The potential interaction between time perception and gaming: A narrative review. *International Journal of Mental Health and Addiction,* 18**,** 1226-1246.

Okumus, B. 2021. A qualitative investigation of Millennials' healthy eating behavior, food choices, and restaurant selection. *Food, Culture & Society,* 24**,** 509-524.

Parekh, N., Khalife, G., Hellmers, N. & D'eramo Melkus, G. 2020. The Healthy Eating and Living Against Noncommunicable Diseases Study: An Innovative Family-Based Intervention. *The Diabetes Educator,* 46**,** 569-579.

Poelman, M. P., Dijkstra, S. C., Sponselee, H., Kamphuis, C., Battjes-Fries, M. C., Gillebaart, M. & Seidell, J. C. 2018. Towards the measurement of food literacy with respect to healthy eating: the development and validation of the self perceived food literacy scale among an adult sample in the Netherlands. *International Journal of Behavioral Nutrition and Physical Activity,* 15**,** 1-12.

Ramadan, R. & Widyani, Y. Game development life cycle guidelines. 2013 International Conference on Advanced Computer Science and Information Systems (ICACSIS), 2013. IEEE, 95-100.

Rober, M. 2018. The Super Mario Effect-Tricking Your Brain into Learning More. *Retrieved,* 5**,** 2019.

Saqib, M., Hisham-Ul-Hassan, K., Shadab, I. & Mehmood, N. 2023. Impact of Academic Stress on Secondary School Student's Performance: A Qualitative Exploration. *Journal of Asian Development Studies,* 12**,** 1068-1079.

Silva, P. 2023. Food and nutrition literacy: Exploring the divide between research and practice. *Foods,* 12**,** 2751.

Takbiri, Y., Bastanfard, A. & Amini, A. 2023. A gamified approach for improving the learning performance of K-6 students using Easter eggs. *Multimedia Tools and Applications,* 82**,** 20683-20701.

Wolfe, A., Louchart, S. & Loranger, B. The impacts of design elements in interactive storytelling in VR on emotion, mood, and self-reflection. International Conference on Interactive Digital Storytelling, 2022. Springer, 616-633.

Author biographies

Nadine du Piesanie, a PhD candidate at the University of Pretoria, researches how gamification can enhance Generation Alpha's food literacy. Her work engages young learners through interactive methods, helping them grasp key concepts in nutrition, food preparation, and sustainability. She explores how gamified strategies improve educational outcomes and long-term food literacy.

Dr. Nadene Marx-Pienaar, a senior lecturer at the University of Pretoria, specialises in sustainable consumption and corporate social responsibility. With extensive experience in hospitality and retail, her research spans food waste reduction, consumer behaviour, and supply chain management. She actively collaborates with industry partners and supervises postgraduate students, contributing to food security initiatives.

Dr. Nadine Sonnenberg is a senior lecturer in the Department of Consumer and Food Science at the University of Pretoria. Her research focuses on consumers' environmentally and socially responsible choice behaviour, specifically addressing issues in emerging market contexts that contribute to or inhibit such behaviour within the apparel and interior goods sector.

Dr. Adeline Pretorius, a dietician with years of clinical experience, joined UP in 2014 as a lecturer. Her research focuses on resting energy expenditure, child nutrition, and dietary interventions to address malnutrition in schools and communities. Her work has been recognised both locally and internationally for its contributions to nutritional science.

Utilzing Mobile Learning and Gamification to Control Tobacco Use in India"

Eve M. Nagler[1,2], Chuck Sigmund[3,] Priyanka Ghosh[4], Smita P. Warke[1], Leah C. Jones[1], Paromita Mehta[3], Samhita Kalidindi[1], Mangesh S. Pednekar[4]
[1]Center for Community-Based Research, Dana-Farber Cancer Institute, Boston, USA
[2]Department of Social and Behavioral Sciences, Harvard T.H. Chan School of Public Health, Boston, USA
[3]ProMobile BI, Temecula, CA, USA
[4] Healis Sekhsaria Institute for Public Health, Navi Mumbai, India
eve_nagler@dfci.harvard.edu
chuck@promobilebi.com
ghoshp@healis.org
smitap_warke@dfci.harvard.edu
leahcarolinej@gmail.com
paromita@promobilebi.com
samhita_kalidindi@dfci.harvard.edu
pednekarm@healis.org

Abstract: The tobacco crisis confronting low- and middle-income countries (LMICs) requires widespread implementation of effective programs, such as *Tobacco Free Teachers-Tobacco Free Society* (TFT-TFS). We demonstrated the efficacy of TFT-TFS in increasing tobacco cessation among teachers in the Indian state of Bihar. To scale TFT-TFS, we are pioneering a smartphone-based mobile learning strategy to train principals in Madhya Pradesh, India to implement and monitor TFT-TFS in schools. Mobile learning offers a flexible, scalable, and cost-effective alternative to in-person training. Strategic use of gamification mechanics and digital storytelling foster a dynamic learning environment to enhance learning outcomes, engagement, and implementation of TFT-TFS's six monthly themes and four program components. The TFT-TFS smartphone training incorporates kite imagery, which in India represents change and healthy competition. Participants navigate each module, engaging with animated videos, digital assessments, and interactive activities. Upon a school's successful completion of each theme, the school's kite receives a new color and teachers' actions as tobacco-free ambassadors give the kite height. The TFT-TFS smartphone training showcases a unique mobile learning application that integrates complex gamification and tests how to scale up an effective tobacco control program in schools in India. The TFT-TFS smartphone training may also have significance to other public health-related training efforts in India and in other LMICs.

1. Introduction

Tobacco-related deaths are rising rapidly in low and middle-income countries (LMICs). India's population is the second largest consumer of tobacco products in the world: 29% of adults smoke and/or use smokeless tobacco and around 1.2 million die annually from tobacco-related causes (Sinha *et al.*, 2014; Jha *et al.*, 2008). India also has the highest oral cancer rate globally (Gupta *et al.*, 2014), along with low cessation rates (Jindal *et al.*, 2006). Reducing tobacco-related mortality in India and other LMICs requires scale-up of effective tobacco control programs—such as *Tobacco-Free Teachers, Tobacco-Free Society* (TFT-TFS)—that leverage the power of community leaders and institutions.

In LMICs, traditional approaches to implementing tobacco control programs involve in-person training (Mormina and Pinder, 2018), which brings logistical challenges and variability in delivery that can affect program integrity (Orfaly *et al.*, 2005). Mobile learning on smartphones may bridge some gaps, through: ready access to audio and video content; real-time data feedback and tracking (Curran *et al.*, 2017); and the ability to access content anytime and anywhere, allowing users to learn at their own pace. Digital content can also be updated and disseminated more quickly and less expensively than printed materials.

Researchers in India and the United States (US) previously demonstrated the success of TFT-TFS in a cluster-randomized study in Bihar, India. Tobacco use cessation rates among teachers in intervention schools were double those of teachers in control schools (Sorensen et al., 2013). TFT-TFS provides tobacco users and non-users with the knowledge and skills to quit or help someone else quit, leveraging teachers' status as societal role models. However, scaling in-person training faces resource limitations and logistical challenges. These obstacles inspired the development of a smartphone-based training that could be implemented broadly, rapidly, and at low cost, especially in rural and under-resourced areas where tobacco use is prevalent.

Grounded in the ubiquity of smartphones across India, the research team is now examining the utility of a gamified smartphone-based training app for program implementers, i.e., school principals (or their designee), in districts of Madhya Pradesh (MP). This initiative aims to determine if principals' implementation of TFT-TFS in their schools following smartphone training will be as good or superior compared to principals receiving in-person training.

2. Infrastructure

Setting: Madhya Pradesh, India's second largest state, has a population of more than 72 million. Approximately 34% of all adults (Tata Institute of Social Sciences, 2018) and 21% of school personnel (Sinha, Gupta and Gangadharan, 2007) in MP use tobacco.

Population: We selected 200 high schools and higher secondary schools across two districts and randomly assigned 110 to receive smartphone training and 90 to receive in-person training.

TFT-TFS program: With the goal of creating a tobacco-free school environment, TFT-TFS is a school-based program for teachers implemented for six months across an academic year. The principal delivers six themes, one-per-month (following an Orientation): i. Teachers as Role Models; ii. Health Effects of Tobacco; iii. Motivation to Quit Tobacco; iv. Skills to Quit Tobacco; v. Dealing with Withdrawal; and vi. Maintenance and Celebration. Each TFT-TFS theme has four core program components:

1. Principal-facilitated theme-based group discussions with teachers
2. Cessation support, including sharing a self-help quit booklet and referrals to government resources
3. Hanging theme-based tobacco control posters
4. Displaying and implementing a school tobacco control policy

Teachers become tobacco-free ambassadors by conducting "bonus activities" including: motivating school and community members to quit; sharing information on the harmful effects of tobacco; and providing cessation resources.

Gamified app development: Utilizing game elements in a non-game environment (Deterding *et al.*, 2011), or **gamification**, increases motivation to complete tasks (Deterding *et al.*, 2011; Werbach and Hunter, 2012). Researchers have identified more than 200 game "mechanics" to engage end users (Peters and Cornetti, 2019) to enhance learning outcomes. In the context of health behavior change, gamification has been shown to encourage participation and program adherence (Cugelman, 2013).

Digital storytelling is a pedagogical approach that (Smeda, Dakich and Sharda, 2010) presents consistent themes, characters, and story throughout the training. Digital storytelling allows learners to: synthesize the material into their understanding of their daily activities; draw conclusions about knowledge application; and identify thematic relationships across training materials. Digital storytelling has been shown to increase participant engagement, reduce time to mastery, and dramatically reduce abandonment rates (Hunter and Hunter, 2006).

To inform app design, we conducted *formative research* via focus groups and interviews with principals and teachers. We explored mobile usage patterns and preferences, technological familiarity, and perceptions of gamification. Almost all participants had Android-based smartphones. They were well-acquainted with teaching apps widely used during COVID-19, and preferred shorter, animated audio-visuals in Hindi. Further, they recommended having a leaderboard to motivate and maintain healthy competition among schools.

We also conducted the Reiss Motivational Profile with six MP principals to reveal what engages them (Reiss, 2013). Principals ranked high on curiosity, honor, idealism, order, and status. Accordingly, we developed strategies to enhance their learning outcomes by tying game mechanics (e.g., a point system) to these specific motivations. The smartphone training thus employs a combination of game mechanics and digital storytelling to immerse and engage participants in the content.

Kite theme: Based on our formative research, we selected a kite-flying motif for our app design and gamification strategy. In Indian society, kite flying symbolizes communal harmony through friendly competition. In the app, each school is represented by a kite. A school's performance is gauged by gains in color and in the height of their school kite.

Cultural relevance: We converted in-person TFT-TFS training content into animated training videos, which allowed the study team to design a creative, customizable, and immersive environment. We also created characters and stories aligned with local MP culture and representation in Hindi.

TFT-TFS training app: The app login screen (Figure 1) features the image of the hypothetical *"Aadarsh Vidyalaya"* (The Ideal School), emphasizing TFT-TFS's aim to help schools become tobacco-free. The app has three sections: (1) The "Principal's Journey" provides access to gamified training content and program components for each theme; (2) the "Teachers' Journey" helps teachers track their bonus activities; and (3) the "Dashboard" displays a school's progress in comparison to other schools.

Figure 1: *Login screen with the idyllic school image*

Principal's Journey: The home page features a map of MP (Figure 2) with the themes plotted on it to simplify navigation. The Orientation at the beginning of the journey provides an overview of TFT-TFS, app features, scoring, navigation, and videos offering insight into tobacco use in India. To assess how well principals understand the content, they take a brief quiz after each video. This process of verifying participant knowledge is repeated throughout the app. Upon completion of the Orientation, the school is awarded a kite divided into six segments, with each segment representing a TFT-TFS theme.

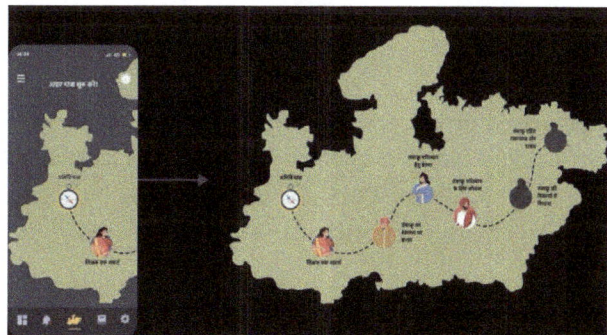

Figure 2: *App home page and the full map of Madhya Pradesh when swiped*

All themes are similarly structured. For instance, in Theme 1, *Shikshak ek Aadarsh* (Teachers as Role Models), principals watch a video about a teacher who

e-Learning Excellence Awards

raises awareness about tobacco's harmful effects after a student drops out due to family circumstances related to tobacco use. After taking a quiz, principals download a guide to facilitate the first group discussion, and instructions for implementing the theme's other three program components. Additionally, the app guides principals in encouraging teachers to conduct bonus activities in the school, family, and community. To document component implementation, the principal completes a form and uploads a photo (e.g., poster on the wall). Once a school completes Theme 1, the school kite gains the color blue, and so on, until the kite is filled in with the six colors representing the six themes.

Each theme's module has its own landing page. Content is organized in a carousel-style display that allows the learner to swipe and see viewed and unviewed content within the theme. Users can navigate back to previous content or activities at any time. The app also delivers weekly push notifications to motivate principals to complete their monthly activities.

Teachers' Journey: Teachers begin by watching videos about TFT-TFS; how the themes are connected to the kite flying; and how schools can score points. Then, teachers conduct bonus activities during each theme with students, friends, family and community members and record their actions on their smartphones.

How schools score points: Implemention of the four core components—alongside teachers' bonus activities—earns schools points and determines a school's standing in the kite flying game. The combination of core and bonus activities within each theme offers schools opportunities to score points, with greater activity completion indicating greater implementation within the school and community.

Dashboard: The dashboard (Figure 3) has four tabs that track each school's progress: Kite Page, Bonus Activities Page, Leaderboard, and Scoreboard. The Kite Page summarizes program component completion per theme. The Bonus Activities Page displays teachers' bonus activities. The Leaderboard displays the top five schools in the district, represented by their kites flying highest in the sky. Finally, the Scoreboard lists all district schools, ranking them based on score.

Figure 3: Dashboard with bonus activities, leaderboard, and school kite

3. Challenges

In designing the TFT-TFS training app, we encountered challenges that became opportunities to improve the app's feasibility and acceptability. For example, principals expressed concerns about the amount of space the app might take on their phones. In response, the team compressed video and images to limit storage space required. Principals also faced internet outages, particularly in very rural areas of MP, so the training content was built natively into the app. This way, users can access the videos without Internet connectivity.

While our India/US team has extensive experience working across India, we had limited knowledge of app usage and internet constraints in rural MP. To gain this contextual understanding, we visited multiple schools and worked with principals to tailor the app for a primarily rural/tribal audience. App modifications included: revising visuals and grammar; adjusting the aesthetics of the animated characters; and making app functionality more efficient. This formative research and subsequent refinements are critical to enhance participant learning outcomes, personal and cultural relevance, and sustainability.

4. How the initiative was received

Comments from principals in a TFT-TFS WhatsApp group suggest anecdotally that they enjoy the healthy competition. As one male principal commented after completing Theme 4, "My school came at 2nd position this time, but I assure you that next theme onwards we will come in the 1st position." Another expressed, "My school's kite is at the first position since the beginning of this program. Our teachers are very motivated with this. Thank you for bringing this program to us." Finally, a female principal expressed her overall satisfaction: "The app and the program are good, and the leaderboard is quite a motivating factor."

5. Learning outcomes

The primary learning objective of this initiative is to determine if principals can implement TFT-TFS in their schools following smartphone-based training.

Measures*:* We will assess implementation of each program component and then examine the percentage of schools implementing all four components. A school will be coded as having successfully implemented the program if: 1) discussions with teachers addressed 3/6 themes; 2) cessation materials were shared with all teachers; 3) at least 3/6 posters were hung; and 4) the tobacco policy was posted. If a school does not meet these criteria, it will be coded as inadequate implementation.

Factors affecting implementation: In August/September 2024, we will qualitatively identify factors underlying observed variations in TFT-TFS program implementation and training app usage. We will select principals and teachers from rural, urban, and tribal schools and DOE leadership to participate in interviews and focus groups. We will invite principals to propose solutions to implementation challenges and recommendations for future use of this e-learning technology.

Findings: We are currently gathering implementation data and expect to have final results by late 2024/early 2025. Preliminary findings indicate that 96/110 (87%) of the principals who received training on the TFT-TFS training app completed the Orientation session. This indicates their ability to download the app, log in, interact with content, and complete quizzes. Quotes above also highlight overall enthusiasm for the app.

6. Plans to further develop the initiative

To our knowledge, this is the first initiative to systematically assess the use of smartphones to train school personnel to deliver and track a tested tobacco control program. Future directions include expanding smartphone training across MP and India. We will also examine how this initiative provides evidence supporting gamified smartphone training and learning models. Finally, we will explore how smartphones can be used to train program implementers to address other health issues in LMICs, such as the rise of non-communicable diseases. This includes assessing technology and learning preferences of the intended audience to build a culturally and linguistically relevant app, and tailoring content for the language/s and health literacy of the user population (Coughlin *et al.*, 2016).

7. Conclusion

The TFT-TFS smartphone training app showcases a unique mobile learning application that integrates complex gamification and tests the potential of this e-learning platform to scale up an effective tobacco control program in schools in India. Further, the smartphone-based training can be adapted to address other health issues in India and in other LMICs.

References

Baker, Angela, Dede, Chris and Evans, Julie (2018), The 8 Essentials for Mobie Learning Success in Education, Qualcomm Wireless Reach, San Diego, CA.
Coughlin, S, Thind, H, Liu, B, Champagne, N, Jacobs, M and Massey, RI (2016), Mobile Phone Apps for Preventing Cancer Through Educational and Behavioral Interventions: State of the Art and Remaining Challenges, *JMIR mHealth and uHealth*, 4, (2), p. e69.
Cugelman, B (2013), Gamification: What It Is and Why It Matters to Digital Health Behavior Change Developers, *JMIR Serious Games*, 1, (1), p. e3.
Curran, V, Matthews, L, Fleet, L, Simmons, K, Gustafson, DL and Wetsch, L (2017), A Review of Digital, Social, and Mobile Technologies in Health Professional Education, *J Contin Educ Health Prof*, 37, (3), 2017/08/24 ed, pp. 195–206.
Deterding, S, Dixon, D, Khaled, R and Nacke, L (2011), From game design elements to gamefulness: defining 'gamification', *Proceedings of the 15th International Academic MindTrek Conference: Envisioning Future Media Environments*, Association for Computing Machinery, New York, NY, USA, pp. 9–15.
Gupta, PC, Ray, CS, Murti, PR and Sinha, DN (2014), Rising incidence of oral cancer in Ahmedabad city, *Indian J Cancer*, 51 Suppl 1, 2014/12/20 ed, pp. S67-72.
Hunter, LP and Hunter, LA (2006), Storytelling as an Educational Strategy for Midwifery Students, *Journal of Midwifery & Women's Health*, 51, (4), pp. 273–278.
Jha, P, Jacob, B, Gajalakshmi, V, Gupta, PC, Dhingra, N, Kumar, R, Sinha, DN, Dikshit, RP, Parida, DK, Kamadod, R, Boreham, J and Peto, R (2008), A nationally representative case-control study of smoking and death in India, *N Engl J Med*, 358, (11), 2008/02/15 ed, pp. 1137–47.
Jindal, SK, Aggarwal, AN, Chaudhry, K, Chhabra, SK, D'Souza, GA, Gupta, D, Katiyar, SK, Kumar, R, Shah, B and Vijayan, VK (2006), Tobacco smoking in India: prevalence, quit-rates and respiratory morbidity, *Indian J Chest Dis Allied Sci*, 48, (1), 2006/02/18 ed, pp. 37–42.
Mormina, M and Pinder, S (2018), A conceptual framework for training of trainers (ToT) interventions in global health, *Globalization and Health*, 14, (1), 2018/10/24 ed, p. 100.
Orfaly, RA, Frances, JC, Campbell, P, Whittemore, B, Joly, B and Koh, H (2005), Train-the-trainer as an educational model in public health preparedness, *J Public Health Manag Pract*, Suppl, 2005/10/06 ed, pp. S123-7.
Peters, J and Cornetti, M (2019), Deliberate Fun: A Purposeful Application of Game Mechanics to Learning Experiences, Sententia Publishing.
Reiss, S (2013), The Reiss Motivation Profile: What Motivates You?, IDS Publishing Corporation.
Sinha, DN, Gupta, PC and Gangadharan, P (2007), Tobacco use among students and school personnel in India, *Asian Pacific journal of cancer prevention: APJCP*, 8, (3), pp. 417–421.

e-Learning Excellence Awards

Sinha, DN, Palipudi, KM, Gupta, PC, Singhal, S, Ramasundarahettige, C, Jha, P, Indrayan, A, Asma, S and Vendhan, G (2014), Smokeless tobacco use: a meta-analysis of risk and attributable mortality estimates for India, *Indian J Cancer*, 51 Suppl 1, 2014/12/20 ed, pp. S73-7.

Smeda, N, Dakich, E and Sharda, N (2010), Developing a Framework for Advancing e-Learning through Digital Storytelling, pp. 169–176.

Sorensen, G, Pednekar, MS, Sinha, DN, Stoddard, AM, Nagler, E, Aghi, MB, Lando, HA, Viswanath, K, Pawar, P and Gupta, PC (2013), Effects of a tobacco control intervention for teachers in India: results of the Bihar school teachers study, *Am J Public Health*, 103, (11), 2013/09/14 ed, pp. 2035–40.

Tata Institute of Social Sciences, M (2018), Global Adult Tobacco Survey GATS 2 India 2016-17, Ministry of Health and Family Welfare, Government of India, New Delhi, India.

Werbach, K and Hunter, D (2012), For the Win: How Game Thinking Can Revolutionize Your Business, Wharton School Press.

Author Biographies

Dr. Eve Nagler is an implementation scientist at Harvard TH Chan School of Public Health and Dana-Farber Cancer Institute. Her research focuses on designing, testing, and implementing theory-driven interventions that optimize the local context. She has worked in public health in Asia, Africa, and the USA for almost 40 years.

Chuck Sigmund, M.S., M.A.Ed is President of ProMobile BI, a multinational technology and L&D company. Chuck's research leans heavily on evaluating the impact and ROI of programs and large-scale initiatives. Throughout his career he has been on the forefront of designing innovative programs to solve difficult business problems.

Using Gamification and Artificial Intelligence to Increase Learning Effectiveness and Motivation

Lam Tai Lee
Lok Sin Tong Leung Kau Kui Primary School (Branch), Hong Kong
ltlee@lst-lkkb.edu.hk

1. Introduction

Hong Kong students are often considered to lack motivation to learn English because classroom activities are based on the routines of teacher-talk and student-listen a.k.a. spoon-feeding education (Cheung, 2001). According to my observations, over half of the target students in the class were low achievers in English. After some investigation, it was believed that they had difficulties with English learning and low motivation for learning English. One possible reason was that they did not learn English effectively in online classes during the class suspension period, resulting in a loose foundation in English grammar and poor English academic results.

For ESL/EFL students to read, write, speak, and understand English effectively, grammar is a vital part of the language. According to Ellis (2006), teaching grammar is unquestionably important for language mastery, and for attaining accuracy and fluency. Yet, grammar is a complicated language variable that is difficult to teach and learn (Hashim et al., 2019). Most grammar classes are designed to fit the traditional teaching style, which is not preferred by ESL students (Chung, 2017). It is doubtful that the traditional practices will help students develop motivation in learning English grammar. In these days, students prefer using mobile technologies in their learning (Byrne-Davis et al., 2015). Therefore, teaching grammar should be fun. In line with the concerns highlighted, gamification in e-learning and generative artificial intelligence can create an enjoyable classroom atmosphere and attract students' attention to learn English.

As the class teacher and English subject teacher of my students, I want to prepare and equip my students to thrive in a world increasingly shaped by AI technologies. Therefore, the blended mode of learning is my approach to e-learning in this initiative. I attempted to design interesting and attractive activities with a wide range of e-learning and generative AI platforms. Although gamification has been the subject of many studies, the study on enhancing grammar mastery using gamification in a primary school context and examining a wide range of e-learning platforms is rarely found.

Figure 1: The design of the instructional strategy

2. The infrastructure

Since the 2018/19 school year, my school has implemented the "Bring Your Own Device" (BYOD) scheme from Primary 4 to 6. Students can bring their tablets to school to enhance e-learning in terms of personalization and flexibility. My school also applies for funding to purchase tablets for loan to needy students. This ensures that all my students have equal opportunities to access e-learning so that my initiative can be implemented effectively. Every teacher at my school is also provided with an iPad to facilitate the use of IT in class. My school not only has adequate computer equipment, but the whole school campus also has access to Wi-Fi and the internet connection is stable. Thus, an IT-supported environment for e-learning is well-established in my school.

To ensure the effective use of learning platforms and applications for e-learning, I actively participate in different e-learning-related events and corresponding trainings. I always explore up-to-date e-learning and AI platforms, such as Blooket, Gimkit, Canva, Playground AI, etc. to assist students with pre-lesson, in-lesson, and post-lesson learning activities. Though most of the e-learning platforms are free to use, we are supported to buy the paid versions for more features and better experiences. My school has reserved adequate funding for the English Department to purchase different e-learning platforms. By the end of each school year, teachers are invited to propose e-learning platforms to purchase in the following school year.

Starting from the 2020/2021 school year, my school has chosen Microsoft Teams to be our Learning and Management System (LMS). To conduct the e-learning activities effectively and efficiently, game links are sent to students in the chat room during lessons. Students can access different game links and learning materials on Teams after school (see Appendix 1). My school also provided a Google account for students. They could use it to log in to different platforms easily.

A small-scale study was conducted in the academic year 2022/2023. I employed gamification in 5 different e-learning platforms in grammar teaching which aimed at increasing students' learning motivation and making grammar learning fun. In selecting the subject, convenience sampling was used. The sample consisted of 21 Primary 5 students from my class. All of them were between 9 to 10 years old at the time of study and their mother tongue was Cantonese. English was introduced to them as a second language from K1 at kindergarten. Regarding the gender of the participants, 13 of them were males and 8 of them were females. They studied in an average class, and they possessed a similar level of English proficiency, which was low to intermediate.

The online gamification that implemented in the teaching of grammar, their features, and how they were used are as follows:

Wordwall

Wordwall is one of the web-based gaming platforms that I use frequently with my students. Teachers can create games with different templates, including arcade-style games. After introducing a grammatical item, these games were played interactively in the lessons and assigned as homework for consolidation.

Kahoot!

Kahoot! is a digital game-based platform where teachers can create lessons and knowledge games with various types of questions. Students can compete with one another in a classic leaderboard. Teachers can convert quizzes into game modes like Treasure Trove and Submarine Squad. I held live games in the classroom and assigned games as homework.

Quizalize

Quizalize is a gamified learning platform that allows teachers to create learning games. It is a web-based game that allows teachers to turn a quiz into various types of games, such as sports, race, battle, and arcade. Students can play a solo or team game. I assigned Quizalize games as a summative assessment.

Blooket

Blooket is another web-based learning platform that is built in a gamified way. It combines quizzes with a range of interesting games that students get to play on their own devices in a self-paced manner. For example, in Cafe mode, students answer questions to earn food to serve customers in the game. I held live games in the classroom and assigned games as homework.

Gimkit

Gimkit is a web-based learning platform that allows teachers to use a set of questions to create a game. Students participate solo or in teams to earn in-game money and they can purchase items for their avatars. I held live games in the classroom and played as a participant with my students together. I also assigned games for students to play at weekends.

Different e-learning platforms were applied in the design of teaching. Table 1 shows the number of exposures in each e-learning platform between February and June 2023, and the question types of the games used.

All the questions in the games were designed by me. Given the fact each English lesson is 35 minutes, I used 1 platform in each lesson as a warm-up activity, consolidation, or assessment. Students took out their devices only when they were told. In most game modes on these platforms (except Wordwall), students answer a set of questions within a time limit (normally for 5-7 minutes). They could encounter the same questions repeatedly and learn from their mistakes, enhancing their comprehension and retention. While playing the games, I walked around the classroom and provided individualized support immediately to students who struggled. At the end of the game, the top students with the highest scores were invited to take a picture with the podium on the big screen. After each game, I reviewed the game report with students and offered immediate feedback. I also adjusted my teaching content based on students' performances.

Table 1: Number of exposures to e-learning platforms and question types used

	Word wall	Kahoot!	Quizalize	Blooket	Gimkit	Total:
Live game (In-lesson):	2	2	0	0	7	11
Assignment (Post-lesson):	6	1	2	2	2	13
Types of questions used	True or false, Multiple choice questions Group sort, Missing word, Whack-a-mole	Multiple choice questions True or false, Puzzle	Multiple choice questions Scrambled letters, True or false	Multiple choice questions, True or false	Multiple choice questions, True or false	

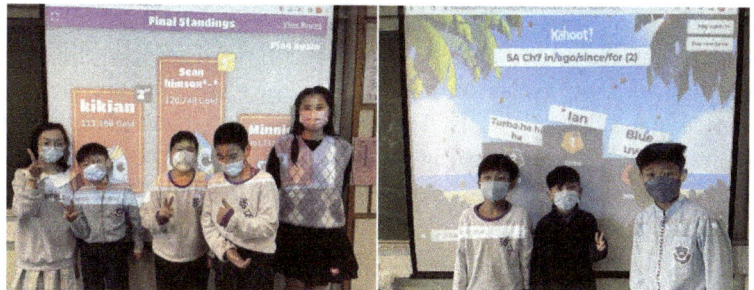

Figure 2: Students taking pictures with the podiums (left: Blooket, right: Kahoot!)

Apart from using gamified e-learning platforms, I introduced various AI platforms to my students this academic year. After students finished a piece of writing, I wanted my students to extend their learning by creating a video using generative AI technology. First, I taught my students to use an AI image generator, Playground AI, to create pictures for their work. Students were taught how to write prompts to create relevant pictures based on their writings. After that, I taught my students to use Canva to make and edit their videos. For example, they added pictures, subtitles, sound effects, and so on. Then I introduced AI voice generators to my students, Voicemaker and Elevenlabs. Students generated text-to-speech voiceovers for their videos. After completing their videos, students were asked to post them on Padlet or Flip. Students could share their videos with the whole class and give "Likes" to each other.

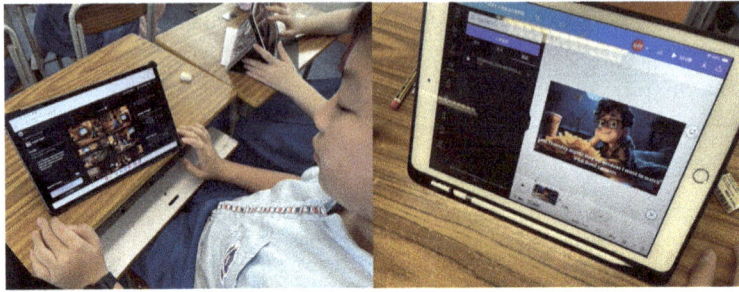

Figure 3: Students using Playground AI (left) and Canva (right)

3. Challenges encountered and how they were overcome

Lack of learning motivation was one of the major challenges encountered initially. One of my colleagues who teaches Mathematics told me that he always played Kahoot! games with his students during the online lessons during the pandemic. Yet, his students were bored of Kahoot! as it was the only gamified platform that he used. My colleague inspired me to adopt a wide range of e-learning platforms in my lesson design. Since my students are Generation Z, I deeply understand their interests. Therefore, I tried to select platforms that could draw their attention. When playing the e-learning games, I often played with my students together in lessons and after classes. For example, Gimkit allows the host to be the player. My students enjoyed playing the games with me and "attacking" me in the game. Another unique feature of Gimkit is that students can create their own questions. My students were happy to be content creators and see their questions appear in the games. When I tried new game modes, my students could learn how to play the games quickly and could even play better than me. I also learnt a lot from my students.

Figure 4: Students and I playing Gimkit

My students always posted screen captures of the leaderboards in the chat room of Teams (see Appendix 2). They wanted to be the champion on the leaderboards. To buy in-game 'clothing' for their avatars (in Gimkit) and collect more avatars (in Blooket), my students were motivated to play the games so that they could earn more in-game money. Apart from competitive games, my students like playing collaborative games (in Kahoot!). I was happy that the more able students could help the lower achievers in the games with flexible seating arrangements.

Though choices were given to my students, I assigned different games at different stages of their learning process. Games were also selected based on students' needs so that I could make sure they could learn effectively while playing the games happily. Apart from that, I formed the routine of using the e-learning platforms with my students. My students knew that games could be their daily homework. These games gradually created a gamified learning environment that positively reinforced my students to persist and overcome challenges. Furthermore, my students had the opportunity to learn from their mistakes and strive for better results by replaying the games I created. This reduced learning anxiety and allowed my students to practice English more freely and confidently.

e-Learning Excellence Awards

4. Students' perceptions about my pedagogical design

The responses collected in the individual interviews revealed that students' motivation toward grammar learning increased after the use of gamification. S1 (a boy), S2 (a girl), and S3 (a boy) were invited for the interviews. Sets of subscales were used for the classification of items under each question for the information collected from the interviewees, including 'Executive Volition', 'Affect', 'Expectation', and 'Value'. The categorization of items is shown in Appendix 3.

Executive Volition

In the interview, Questions 7 and 8 asked for the interviewees' Executive Volition using gamified e-learning platforms to learn English grammar. All responses were positive. All interviewees said that they were willing to play the same English game. S1 and S3 said that they could get a higher rank on the leaderboard if they kept playing the same game. S3 stated, "I can get better results in the games. I want to beat my classmates on the leaderboard." They also said that they would like to play more games to learn about English grammar in the future. S1 stated, "I want more games because I can know the correct answers immediately when I play a game. I think games are more interesting than worksheets." S3 supported, "I prefer playing games rather than doing worksheets." Furthermore, S2 stated that she would like more games because they are exciting, and they help her learn grammar better.

Affect

All interviewees had positive Affects in learning English grammar with gamification. They all expressed that they liked to learn grammar in a gamified way. When asking for the interviewees' perceptions directly using adjectives, all the comments were positive. The following were some commonly appeared positive adjectives (with frequencies in parentheses): excited (3), happy (2), stimulating (1), joyful (1), thrilled (1) and interesting (1). All interviewees choose Gimkit as their favourite game to learn grammar. When asked to explain further, S1 stated that he enjoys playing games that allow cooperation with other classmates. S2 stated, "I like the *Snowy Survival* in Gimkit because it is exciting!" S3 stated, "Because I can control my avatar in Gimkit and it is exciting."

Expectation

Regarding the aspect of Expectation, all interviewees agreed that it made learning English grammar easier after playing games on e-learning platforms. They also agreed that the use of gamification in grammar teaching could enhance their academic results. The findings aligned with the results of the examinations.

Value

Regarding the Value of learning English grammar, the findings displayed positive results. All interviewees agreed that mastering English grammar is important for them. S1 pointed out that when visiting the UK, he could communicate with people there. S2 supported, "When visiting English-speaking countries, you can't communicate with people there if you don't know English." S3 stated, "When traveling abroad, I can communicate with others using English." As found in the interviews, all students stated that mastering English was important because it was a means of communication with foreigners. The findings affirmed the importance of grammar learning.

Students' motivation of learning English grammar was also investigated with the pre- and post-questionnaires. The results are plotted in Table 2. Sets of subscales were used for the classification of items under each statement for the information collected from questionnaires, including 'Executive Volition', 'Affect', 'Expectation', and 'Value'. The categorization of items can be seen in Appendix 4.

Table 2: Students' motivation in learning English grammar before and after the study

Subscales of motivation	Pre-questionnaire		Post-questionnaire		Gain
	Mean	SD	Mean	SD	
Executive Volition	3.96	0.86	4.10	0.77	0.14
Affect	3.74	0.92	4.07	0.88	0.33
Expectation	3.40	0.33	3.77	0.88	0.37
Value	3.82	0.90	4.03	0.94	0.21

Table 2 shows the mean gains for Executive Volition and Affect were 0.14 and 0.33. The level of students' Executive Volition increased after using gamification. More students had positive Affects in learning English grammar after the implementation of gamified teaching. In addition, it shows the mean gains for Expectation and Value were 0.37 and 0.21. Students' Expectations in grammar learning increased with gamification. Regarding the Value of learning English grammar, the findings displayed positive results. It had the highest mean gain among the four subscales. More students valued the usefulness of mastering grammar after the use of gamification. The results of the questionnaires suggest that teaching grammar with the use of gamification is more motivating than the traditional way of grammar teaching.

e-Learning Excellence Awards

My students kept asking me if they had a game to play in nearly every lesson. They were more engaged when gamification was adopted. They played English games on their devices actively and they were willing to share and help each other. My students expressed joy and satisfaction when they witnessed their own stories transform from a piece of writing to a video with narrations and subtitles.

Since my students enjoy playing Blooket and Gimkit games and have proven to increase their motivation and learning effectiveness, I decided to promote these two gaming platforms to other classes. In June 2023, I held the first inter-class Gold Quest Competition on Blooket with the whole P.5. It was the first time in my school that over 100 students played on a gamified platform at the same time. My students were eager to be helpers to teach students from other classes to play the game. They were thrilled as they could beat the students from the elite classes. All the students were excited, and my colleagues said that they would try this platform in their lessons.

Figure 5: Inter-class competition on Blooket

At the end of this school year, a questionnaire was given to my student asking their views on the e-learning and AI platforms. Most students agree that artificial intelligence can make English learning more fun. They also agreed that learning generative AI can help them to learn English better and prepare for the future. They expressed that they wanted to learn more about e-learning and AI platforms in the future. Table 3 shows that e-learning and AI platforms can increase students' learning effectiveness and motivation in English.

Table 3: Results of students' learning effectiveness and motivation in English (Academic year 2023/2024)

Questions		Average
1.	E-learning platforms can help you to improve your academic performance in English.	4.4
2.	E-learning platforms can help you understand your mistakes in English.	4.5
3.	E-learning platforms can help you identify your weaknesses in English.	4.55
4.	E-learning platforms can motivate you to learn English.	4.7
5.	I enjoy English lessons with the use of different e-learning platforms.	4.45
6.	I feel a sense of success in English when I perform well in the e-learning platforms.	4.35
7.	Learning generative AI can help you to learn English better.	4.1
8.	Learning generative AI can help you prepare for the future.	4.2
9.	Artificial intelligence can make English learning more fun.	4.3
10.	You want to learn more about e-learning and AI platforms in the future.	4.4

Key: 1: strongly disagree; 5: strongly agree, N=20

5. The learning outcomes

Pre- and delay post-grammar tests were given to students to evaluate the effectiveness of grammar learning before and after the research. The test was about the present perfect tense. Based on the grammar test results, the use of gamification improved the effectiveness of the participants' grammar learning. Table 4 shows the mean scores in pre- and delay post-grammar tests. The average delay post-test result (24.2) after applying the gamification approach is greater than the average results of the pre-test (20.6). The mean gain was 3.6.

Table 4: Mean scores of pre- and delay post-grammar tests (Note. The full mark of the test is 27.)

Aspect description	Pre-test	Delay post-test
Number of students	21	21
Total scores	433.5	509.5
Mean	20.6	24.2
SD	7.22	4.94

Table 5 shows the changes in scores in pre- and delay post-grammar tests. All 21 participants were categorized into 3 groups (low, intermediate, and high English proficiency levels) according to their results in the pre-grammar test. It was found that the number of students in the high English proficiency group increased double from 8 to 16.

e-Learning Excellence Awards

Table 5: Changes of scores in pre- and delay post-grammar tests (Note. The full mark of the test is 27.)

English proficiency levels (scores)	Number of students (Pre-test)	Number of students (Delay post-test)	Changes (Number of students)
Low (0-14)	4	1	-3
Intermediate (15-24)	15	4	-11
High (25-27)	8	16	+8

The use of gamification improved the effectiveness of primary school students' grammar learning in Hong Kong. Gamification had a long-lasting impact on the acquisition of the present perfect tense among students. Students were able to maintain the results in the delay post-test after two months.

Students' performances in the grammar part of the examination were used as one of the data collection instruments. The weighting of grammar accounted for 40% of the whole paper. 29 marks of the questions in grammar were related to the present perfect tense as it was the focus of the exam. Based on the examination results, the use of gamification improved the effectiveness of the participants' grammar learning. Tables 6, 7, and 8 display students' results in grammar of Exams 1, 2, and 3. In Exam 1, only 11 students from my class (5C) got 60 or above. In Exam 2, the participants performed well in grammar as all of them got 60 or above. About 90% of them scored 80-100. Most of my students continued to perform well in grammar in Exam 3. Compared with the results of the other two average classes, my class performed better in grammar. One possible reason was that Class 5D and 5E did not apply gamification in teaching.

Table 6: Statistics of P.5 Grammar in 22/23 English Exam 1 Paper

Score	5A		5B		5C		5D		5E		Whole Form		Pass Rate
80-100	29	96.7%	18	72.0%	8	338.1%	1	5.0%	0		49.1%		67.5%
70-79	0		5	20.0%	2	9.5%	2	10.0%	4	22.2%	11.4%		
60-69	1	3.3%	0		1	4.8%	4	10.0%	2	11.1%	7.0%		
40-59	0		2	8.0%	4	19.0%	5	25.0%	5	27.8%	14.0%		Failure Rate
20-39	0		0		5	3.8%	4	20.0%	5	27.8%	12.3%		32.5%
0-19	0		0		1	4.8%	4	20.0%	2	11.1%	6.1%		
Total	30	100.0%	25	100.0%	21	100.0%	20	100.0%	18	100.0%	114		100.0%

Lam Tai Lee

Table 7: Statistics of P.5 Grammar in 22/23 English Exam 2 Paper

Score	5A		5B		5C		5D		5E		Whole Form	Pass Rate
80-100	29	100.0%	24	100.0%	19	90.5%	13	65.0%	13	65.0%	86.0%	89.5%
70-79	0		0		1	4.8%	1	5.0%	0		1.8%	
60-69	0		0		1	4.8%	1	5.0%	0		1.8%	
40-59	0		0		0		2	10.0%	5	25.0%	6.1%	Failure Rate
20-39	0		0		0		3	15.0%	0		2.6%	10.5%
0-19	0		0		0		0		2	10.0%	1.8%	
Total	29	100.0%	24	100.0%	21	100.0%	20	100.0%	20	100.0%	114	100.0%

Table 8: Statistics of P.5 Grammar in 22/23 English Exam 3 Paper

Score	5A		5B		5C		5D		5E		Whole Form	Pass Rate
80-100	24	80.0%	16	64.0%	14	66.7%	0		4	20.0%	50.0%	74.1%
70-79	5	16.7%	5	20.0%	3	14.3%	3	15.0%	2	10.0%	15.5%	
60-69	1	3.3%	2	8.0%	0		3	15.0%	4	20.0%	8.6%	
40-59	0		2	8.0%	0		6	30.0%	1	5.0%	7.8%	Failure Rate
20-39	0		0		3	14.3%	6	30.0%	5	25.0%	12.1%	25.9%
0-19	0		0		1	4.8%	2	10.0%	4	20.0%	6.0%	
Total	30	100.0%	25	100.0%	21	100.0%	20	100.0%	20	100.0%	116	100.0%

As an English, ICT and Visual Arts teacher, I attempted to integrate English, ICT, and Visual Arts curriculum with cutting-edge Artificial Intelligence tools. Cross-curricular learning not only can help students develop subject knowledge and generic skills, but also their capabilities to integrate all of them. To make a video, students learnt to use AI image generator to create pictures for their stories. They learnt to enter accurate English prompts so that they could generate the pictures that they wanted. They also learnt different video editing techniques by using Canva. The videos that they created were of high quality and their creativity was out of my imagination. The YouTube link below shows one of my students' good work. https://youtu.be/h0BZ49BRRCg

6. Conclusion and plans to further develop the initiative

In this initiative, the importance of adopting all rounded approach of using diverse gamified e-learning platforms was shown. I took gamification to the next level with an innovative pedagogical design. There is a high level of student-teacher interaction and a strong student-teacher relationship in the teaching and learning process. Competition is a crucial game element that highly motivates students to engage in gamification tasks (Sepehr and Head, 2013). For instance, I always played games with students on e-learning platforms. The target students were eager to compete against me and shared their results on LMS with me. When I tried new game modes on the platforms, my students could learn how to play the games quickly and could even play better than me. I also learnt a lot from my students.

It is very feasible for other subject teachers, secondary schools, and even universities to adopt the gamified e-learning platforms that I used. To arouse students' interest in learning, Gimkit and Blooket were found to be the most popular among my students. These platforms are user-friendly and free to use. Teachers can use or customize existing games created by teachers around the world. With a variety of game types and modes, different learning styles can be catered. Furthermore, replacing traditional paper homework and quizzes with digital homework and assessments (games) could motivate students through first-hand observation. It was suspected that the students would experience less academic pressure because the game experience blinded the students to the fact that they were being assessed. Generally, students will be more willing to attempt when facing challenging questions in games. Teachers can make good use of gamification to consolidate and test students' subject knowledge. By using Canva and various generative AI tools, students can visualize their ideas and integrate different skills, making writing more interesting and relevant.

My school has been invited by the Hong Kong Education Bureau to be the IT in Education Centre of Excellence (CoE) to provide e-learning support for other local primary schools. I have held Professional Development Programmes to share my experiences with in-service teachers and provided on-site support services to schools on the implementation of e-learning in English education. I also had experience sharing with undergraduate and postgraduate students. I will continue to promote the pedagogical design and e-learning platforms used in the initiative.

To arouse students' interest in learning, it is suggested that teachers should incorporate more than one e-learning platform. Teachers should be open-minded to explore and use different e-learning tools that suit the needs of their students in teaching. It is also important for teachers to understand the interests of their students so that they can create games that are relevant and engaging to students. Since my students are Generation Z, I deeply understand their interests. They like playing computer and mobile games. Therefore, I tried to select platforms and tools that can draw their attention. I applied gamification in my daily teaching routine and the students were familiar with the e-learning platforms that I used. Choices were offered for my students to select the platforms and game types that they wanted because students had different preferences.

Honestly speaking, it took me a lot of time to make games on different gamified e-learning platforms. I was glad my students' attitudes towards English language learning became positive in these 2 years. Not only did my students gain satisfaction, but so did I when I witnessed my passive students get actively engaged in the learning process through the innovative use of different e-learning and AI platforms. Though the use of gamified e-learning platforms has a lot of advantages, it will not replace the traditional mode of learning. Both are complementing each other under the new normal. Both teachers and students must adjust their mindsets, master the use of different e-learning tools, and keep up with the latest development in technology. By applying the blended learning model, gamification can be combined with face-to-face teaching to maximize learning effectiveness.

Acknowledgments

I would like to thank my school and my principal Ms. Lau Tit Mui who contributed financially and made it possible for me to present this case history at ECEL2024.

References

Byrne-Davis, L., Dexter, H., Hart, J., Cappelli, T., Byrne, G., Sampson, I., Mooney, J., & Lumsden, C. (2015) Just-in-time research: a call to arms for research into mobile technologies in higher education. Research in Learning Technology, 23. https://doi.org/10.3402/rlt.v23.25653

Cheung, C. K. (2001) The use of popular culture as a stimulus to motivate secondary students' English learning in Hong Kong. ELT Journal, 55, 55–61. http://dx.doi.org/10.1093/elt/55.1.55

Chung, S. (2017) A Communicative Approach to Teaching Grammar: Theory and Practice. The English Teacher, 34, 33–50.

Ellis, N. C. (2006) Cognitive perspectives on SLA: The Associative-Cognitive CREED. AILA Review, 19, 100-121.

Hashim, H., Rafiq, R. M., & Md Yunus, M. (2019) Improving ESL Learners' Grammar with Gamified-Learning. Arab World English Journal (AWEJ) Special Issue on CALL, (5). https://doi.org/10.24093/awej/call5.4

e-Learning Excellence Awards

Sepehr, S. and Head, M. (2013) Competition as an element of gamification for learning: an exploratory longitudinal investigation. In Proceedings of Gamification. Stratford, Ontario, Canada, pp.2–8.

Appendix 1

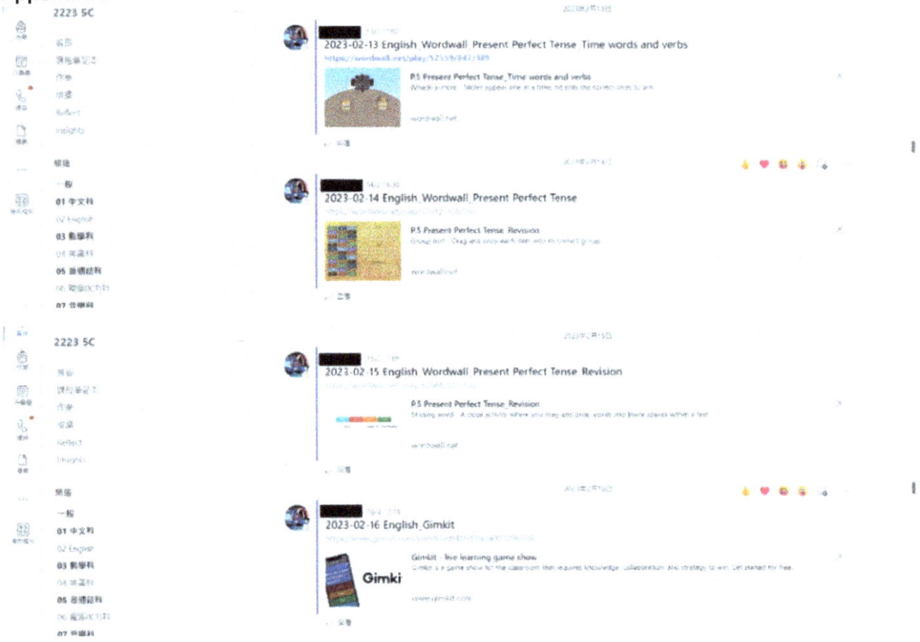

Appendix 2

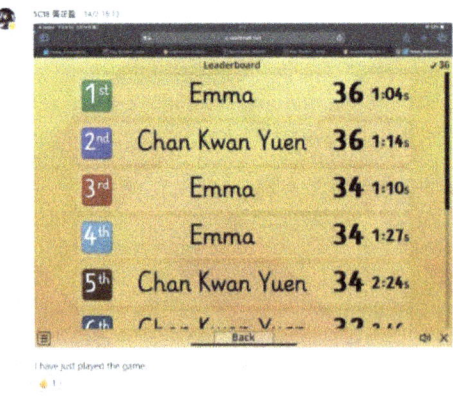

Appendix 3
Categorization of interview items

Subscales	Items	
Executive Volition	Q.7	Are you willing to play the same English grammar game?
	Q.8	Would you like to play more games to learn about English grammar in the future? Why?
Affect	Q.1	Do you like to learn English grammar in a gamified way? Why?
	Q.2	Can you use three adjectives to describe how you feel when I teach English grammar in a gamified way?
	Q.3	What is your favourite game to learn English grammar? Why?
Expectation	Q.4	Does playing games make it easier for you to learn English grammar? Why?
	Q.5	Do you think gamification can enhance your English academic results? Why?
Value	Q.6	Do you think mastering English grammar is important? Why?

Appendix 4
Categorization of questionnaire items

Subscales	Items	
Executive Volition	Q.1	I pay attention in the English lessons when learning grammar.
	Q.5	I hope I can learn more about grammar in the English lessons.
	Q.9	I am willing to try my best to learn English grammar.
Affect	Q.2	Learning English grammar makes me happy.
	Q.6	I think learning English grammar is interesting.
	Q.10	I like learning English grammar.
Expectation	Q.3	I think the questions in the grammar part of the English exams are easy.
	Q.7	I am confident to master English grammar.
	Q.11	I think I can get high marks in the grammar part of the English exams.
Value	Q.4	I think mastering English grammar is useful for me.
	Q.8	I think mastering English grammar is important for me.
	Q.12	I think mastering English grammar can help me master English.

Author Biography

Lam Tai Lee (Master of Teaching with Distinction) is a primary school teacher at Lok Sin Tong Leung Kau Kui Primary School (Branch) in Hong Kong. He started teaching in 2017. He teaches English Language, Visual Arts, and Information and Communications Technology. He has won several e-learning awards from the University of Hong Kong

www.ingramcontent.com/pod-product-compliance
Lightning Source LLC
Chambersburg PA
CBHW072200160426
43197CB00012B/2462